BUS
STO

The First

cc:M

**DO NOT REMOVE
CARDS FROM POCKET**

The First Book of

cc:Mail™

Dan Derrick

SAMS

A Division of Macmillan Computer Publishing

11711 North College, Carmel, Indiana 46032 USA

This book is dedicated to computer users just discovering electronic mail. You now have the world at your fingertips.

International Standard Book Number: 0-672-27383-7
Library of Congress Catalog Card Number: 91-62666

94 93 92 91   8 7 6 5 4 3 2 1

Interpretation of the printing code: the rightmost number of the first series of numbers is the year of the book's printing; the rightmost number of the second series of numbers is the number of the book's printing. For example, a printing code of 91-1 shows that the first printing of the book occurred in 1991.

Screen reproductions in this book were created by means of the program Collage Plus from Inner Media, Inc., Hollis, NH.

Printed in the United States of America

Publisher
Richard K. Swadley

Associate Publisher
Marie Butler-Knight

Managing Editor
Marjorie Hopper

Development Editor
Gregg Bushyeager

Manuscript Editor
John E. Spence

Production Editor
Elizabeth Keaffaber

Cover Artist
Held & Diedrich Design

Indexer
Susan VandeWalle

Production Team
*Claudia Bell, Mike Britton, Brook Farling, Joelynn Gifford, Sandy
Grieshop, Dennis Hager, Debbie Hanna, Audra Hershman, Betty Kish,
Laurie Lee, Diana Moore, Cindy L. Phipps, Tad Ringo, Dennis Sheehan,
Bruce Steed, Jenny Watson*

***Special thanks to Mark Fellows for assuring the technical
accuracy of this book.***

Contents

viii

Introduction

With electronic mail you have tapped into a new channel of communication. You can send and receive messages with the stability of written memos and the ease of telephone conversations. Because you do not hear the receiver's response as you do on the phone, you must create clearly worded messages. And, because incoming messages won't be dropped on your desk like mail, you must remember to "call" your electronic mailbox to pick up your messages.

This book helps you learn about this new method of communication and the tool to use it—cc:Mail. In particular, as you progress through the chapters you will accomplish the following:

- ▶ You will gain a perspective on the advantages and disadvantages of electronic mail, or *e-mail*.
- ▶ You will use Quick Steps to accomplish specific tasks in cc:Mail.
- ▶ You will discover additional features in cc:Mail that save time and enhance your messages.
- ▶ You will learn about e-mail etiquette.
- ▶ You will read messages from other cc:Mail users that explain how they use electronic mail.

> **Tip:** This book does not cover the Macintosh versions of cc:Mail. If you have the OS/2 version, you will find its features and functions are identical to those in the DOS version.

Who This Book Is For

This book is designed as written documentation for all cc:Mail users. Because cc:Mail is a network program, it is installed on a central, or *host*, computer. Your system administrator pays for each individual addressee, or user, on the network, but that price does not include a manual for each user.

cc:Mail User

First-time cc:Mail users will find Quick Steps for many of the cc:Mail actions they want to perform, such as reading and sending messages and managing mailing lists. Although each cc:Mail post office may be arranged differently, this book will help you understand those differences and communicate with ease with any post office.

xiv

Experienced users will find tips and cautions they may not have discovered yet. Special "messages" from other cc:Mail users around the country are included as well. These messages provide perspectives on the ways in which other people use cc:Mail. Experienced users may also find that they can help a novice by suggesting specific sections of this book to read.

The cc:Mail Administrator

First-time cc:Mail administrators will learn the basics of setting up a system. If you are new to networks or electronic mail, this book can provide the information you need to set up the post office and create addresses.

As the system administrator you will need to maintain the post office. This involves adding and deleting users, public mailing lists, and bulletin boards. You are also likely to be called on for help, and this book will provide you with ideas about user support and training as well as innovative methods for using cc:Mail as a communications tool.

What This Book Contains

Each chapter focuses on one aspect of the cc:Mail program. For your convenience, chapters begin with a short list of the main points to be covered and end with a summary of what you learned.

In addition, each chapter contains special features, marked with graphic "icons," to make it easier for you to learn cc:Mail.

 Quick Steps summarize specific steps that allow you to use each feature of cc:Mail immediately. A summary of the Quick Steps in this book is contained on the inside front cover.

1. The left column explains the step to take.

The right column describes the result of that action. ☐

 Tip: Tips are shortcuts or suggestions about a procedure or menu choice.

 Caution: Cautions alert you to possible problems or steps that lead to permanent changes.

 Messages are actual cc:Mail messages sent from other users that include unique hints for using cc:Mail.

This book also uses some special typefaces and symbols. Menu choices and messages displayed on the screen are shown in `computer type`, which looks like the typeface on a computer screen. Anything that you need to type appears as `bold computer type`, with variables indicated in *lowercase italics*. When a menu choice can be selected with just one letter, that letter is capitalized, as in A. Likewise, special keys like the Enter and Backspace keys are capitalized. Special key combinations like the Alt key and the F9 key are shown as Alt-F9, which means to hold down on the Alt key while pressing the F9 key. Some of these key combinations are active even when other programs are running. These are called *hotkey* combinations.

How To Use This Book

If you are new to cc:Mail, read the book in the order presented. Set a goal of covering a chapter a day. In a little more than a week, you'll be an accomplished cc:Mail user.

By referring to the list of Quick Steps on the inside front cover, you can quickly find the steps you need to accomplish a specific goal.

Use Post-It notes to mark sections you refer to frequently. Make a small note on the tab for instant access to those parts of the book. Also, make notes in the book next to the Quick Steps. By doing so you will remember how to use your current version of cc:Mail in the context of your particular post office.

E-Mail Overview

Electronic mail is a way to send messages to other users on your mailing list. Typically this means that your computer is *networked*, or connected, to a host computer, which contains the post office where you send messages. The recipient must either use the same software (in this case cc:Mail) to read those messages or be accessible through a *gateway* on the local system, which forwards messages to foreign e-mail systems.

The information contained in the messages is encoded. No one but the sender, receiver, and system administrator can read those messages. If the data on the network host computer is backed up regularly and the backups are kept, even messages you delete may still exist somewhere in the backup copies of the network data files. If you are concerned about the privacy of your messages, ask your system administrator about the company policy regarding e-mail messages.

E-mail can also function on a global scale, but you still need a common meeting place. Somewhere a computer must contain the post office through which you send and receive your messages. Different remote message services (post offices) are now available, including CompuServe and MCI Mail. Although separate, even these systems are beginning to work together. Users can now pass messages between these systems provided they know the recipients' electronic addresses. The cc:Mail Gateway program can help tie these systems together. Gateway can exchange messages with other cc:Mail post offices and with additional cc:Mail programs, MCI Mail, fax machines, mainframe message services, and others.

Wherever you send messages, you need to follow the basic rules of electronic mail, what's known as e-mail etiquette. Just as it is impolite to hang up the phone without saying "goodbye," it is inconsiderate to write a terse response without referring to the original message: "OK with me." Modern phone equipment rarely requires yelling into the phone. In the world of e-mail, sending messages IN ALL UPPERCASE is the same as SHOUTING ON THE PHONE. As you'll learn in this book, you should always be aware of what your e-mail messages say about you.

xvii

What about your misspelled words in a message? Can you forward mail to someone without the original sender's consent? Can you look at the bulletin board messages of another work group? Although the Emily Post of e-mail has not yet appeared, with this book you can still find answers to these and other questions of electronic mail etiquette.

Write your name in this book. Put it where you can easily find it. Read it and practice using cc:Mail. You are on the leading edge of the information revolution, and you can use electronic mail to make the most of it.

Acknowledgments

This book demonstrates the utility and flexibility of the electronic word. It was composed and edited completely on the computer, and hardly anything appeared on paper until it rolled off the printing press. The ideas were passed along (and enhanced significantly) by Gregg Bushyeager, Development Editor, and John Spence, Manuscript Editor. Contributions were made electronically by cc:Mail users Andy Pickett, Chuck Stegman, and Nick Cutry. Thanks also to

Marie Butler-Knight, Publishing Manager, who put the ideas and people together to make this a book. Diane Braga and Mark Fellows served as contacts with cc:Mail, a division of Lotus Development Corporation. Linda Blevens at CBIS and Kelly Christenson at Novell provided network software.

It's difficult to name everyone else who was a part of this book. Marj Hopper, Managing Editor, and Sam Eudaly, Editorial Assistant, were undoubtedly pushing and pulling at the right times to form these words into a book. And, last, but not least, the folks from the production department listed on the copyright page deserve their due share of thanks for converting these electronic words into a book. Thanks one and all.

Trademarks

xviii

All terms mentioned in this book that are known to be trademarks or service marks are listed below. In addition, terms suspected of being trademarks or service marks have been appropriately capitalized. SAMS cannot attest to the accuracy of this information. Use of a term in this book should not be regarded as affecting the validity of any trademark or service mark.

cc:Mail is a trademark of the Lotus Development Corporation.

CompuServe Incorporated is a registered trademark of H&R Block, Inc.

EtherNet is a trademark of 3Com Corporation.

Hercules Graphics Card is a trademark of Hercules Computer Technology.

HP is a registered trademark of Hewlett-Packard Corporation.

LaserJet is a trademark of Hewlett-Packard Corporation.

Lotus and 1-2-3 are registered trademarks of Lotus Development Corporation.

MCI Mail is a registered trademark of MCI Communications Corporation.

MS-DOS, Microsoft, and Microsoft Windows are registered trademarks of Microsoft Corporation.

PC Paintbrush IV Plus is a registered trademark of ZSoft, Inc.

Publisher's Paintbrush 2.0 is a trademark of ZSoft Corporation.

Quattro Pro is a registered trademark of Borland International, Inc.

UNIX is a registered trademark of AT&T Laboratories.

xix

Getting Started with cc:Mail

In This Chapter

▶ *Basic e-mail concepts and terms*
▶ *An overview of DOS and Windows*
▶ *DOS and Windows with cc:Mail*
▶ *Password ideas and cautions*

Before working with a new software program, you need to know a few basic concepts and terms. Although cc:Mail has fairly standard menus and several ways to make selections from those menus, you may not yet know the basics of sending and receiving electronic mail.

E-mail Basics

Your goal when using cc:Mail is to transmit a message to another user in your cc:Mail *post office*. (Post office and other terms in italics are defined in the next section, "Concepts and Terms.") This message can contain more than just text. For example, you can send graphic images that you've drawn or captured from another program. You can also send DOS files, and you can even attach fax files to each message.

In other words, these messages can be considered packages containing many different items. Each message can contain up to 20 items you create or attach. When the message is received, text and graphic items can be viewed and saved, and DOS files can be copied to the recipient's disk.

Like memos, these messages can be stored in *folders* that you label within the cc:Mail system. You can copy the messages to your own disk, print them out, or delete them. Once stored in your folders, old messages can be retrieved by searching for names, dates, and key words. You'll open, work with, and delete folders as needed.

To make sending messages easier, the *addresses* in your post office are listed. To send a message, you select a name from the list, and the message is automatically addressed. To send the same message to more than one person, you select additional names. Once you have selected the addresses, you type a note, attach files if needed, and send the message. The recipient can "pick up" the message almost immediately.

To send messages to a group of people, you can create *mailing directories*. You choose a name for the list and select the names of individuals in that list. Then you address the message to the list instead of the individuals. Similarly, your system administrator can create public mailing lists for everyone to use.

The messages you send and receive are private, viewable only by you and the recipients, and by the system administrator. Public messages are displayed on *bulletin boards*, which are created by the system administrator. Everyone can read, reply, and copy the messages on a bulletin board. Because cc:Mail tracks all the messages you have read, you can easily see which messages on the bulletin boards you have not yet looked at.

cc:Mail is a powerful tool for communication. When starting with this program, you should first learn which menu choices to make to send and read mail and then how to save messages and forward replies. Once you are familiar with the mechanics of using cc:Mail, you can begin to experience the real power of communicating through electronic mail.

How does electronic mail help you with your work?

Couldn't live without it! It allows me to communicate with people throughout the world and to get updates and follow trends. I also receive questions from the field via cc:Mail.

Electronic mail has greatly reduced my use of the phone and internal mail systems. I am now able to converse electronically with my colleagues. The ability to maintain mailing lists and archive threads of conversations has improved my ability to manage frequently needed information. Remote access means never being out of touch with the office. Very nice for the part of the country that I live and work in!

Concepts and Terms

3

Post Office

The e-mail post office is similar in format to your local U.S. Post Office. Each individual has a unique address. When messages come in, they are placed in that individual's electronic mailbox. When the recipient "checks in" at the post office, those messages are waiting to be picked up.

In computer terms the post office resembles a database. It contains a list of addresses (user names), a list of groups, and a list of bulletin boards, and it stores messages as well. To access these lists and read messages you need to use an electronic mail program such as cc:Mail.

System Administrator

The system administrator installs and manages the post office on the network. This includes creating all mailboxes, group lists, and bulletin boards. The administrator also uses additional software tools to monitor message traffic and back up the files. If a problem occurs with the network, the administrator is responsible for finding the solution.

Although the administrator can change user passwords, he or she cannot do so without the user's knowledge. However, it is assumed that, under normal circumstances, the administrator will respect users' privacy.

Mailboxes

To receive mail at a post office an individual must have a mailbox that has the user's name as the local mailing address. The system administrator purchases one or more User Packs to increase the number of users. Although less expensive, the User Pack does not provide a manual for each user.

Inbox

When messages are received at the post office, they are placed in the Inbox of the addressed users. Just like an inbox tray on your desk, this Inbox holds the message until you determine what to do with it. When you run cc:Mail, the opening screen shows how many messages you have in your Inbox and how many are still unread.

Mailing Directory

4

All users with access to the post office are kept in the mailing directory. These names can be added by the system administrator only up to the number allowed by cc:Mail User Packs. The directory is alphabetical and may list either first names or last names first, depending on the administrator's preference. The directory may also have aliases (nicknames) for users on the list, which can make it easier to locate a user.

Bulletin Boards

Bulletin boards are established by the system administrator and provide public addresses for sending messages and files of interest to other users. Others may or may not choose to read the messages depending on their interest in the bulletin board topic.

The messages on bulletin boards share some characteristics with private messages in that they can include files and graphics elements. But there are no restrictions on who can read bulletin board messages.

Mailing Lists

The administrator may create mailing lists for general use. These can be designed to direct messages to everyone in a department or to everyone with a specific job title. Anyone can use the public mailing lists, and you can also create your own private mailing lists.

Folders

Each message you receive can be copied to one or more folders. You create and name up to 200 folders for these messages. Each folder can contain up to 1,600 messages. The folder names can contain up to 30 characters and might be based on the names of specific projects or specific individuals. All messages stored in folders are kept in the same physical location as the post office on the network host computer.

Archive Files

Messages from the Inbox, folders, or bulletin boards can be copied to the local or network disk as archive files. These files are kept in the special cc:Mail format and cannot be used or viewed by any other program. If you save the archive files to the network disk, anyone else with access to that disk can also read and use your archive files by using cc:Mail.

5

The cc:Mail Programs

The cc:Mail package actually contains several programs. The main program is called the Mail program. It is used from the operating system and allows you to perform all the cc:Mail functions. Additional programs provide other ways to use this e-mail system.

Messenger

The Messenger program allows you to send and receive mail while you are using another program. It also notifies you when you receive a new message.

You must load Messenger before starting another program. Then you can press Alt-2 to pop up a small window over your other program, as shown in Figure 1.1. From this window you can read Inbox messages or send messages. Some of the cc:Mail features are missing in this smaller version. For example, when moving an Inbox message to a folder in Messenger, you must know the name of the folder, since you will not see a list of folders to select from. Messenger also does not provide help through the F1 key.

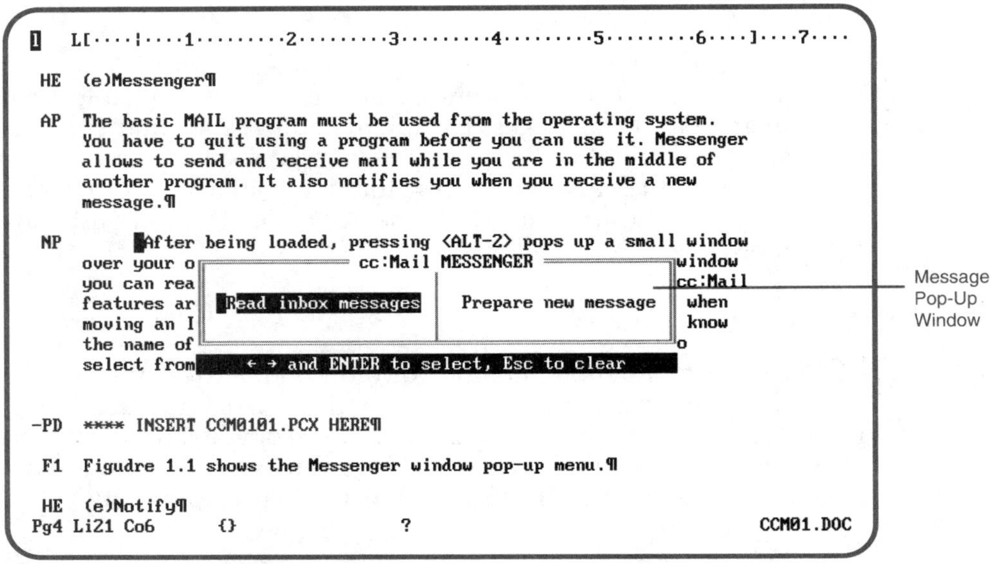

```
◻    L[····⌐····1·········2·········3·········4·········5········6····]····7····

HE   (e)Messenger¶

AP   The basic MAIL program must be used from the operating system.
     You have to quit using a program before you can use it. Messenger
     allows to send and receive mail while you are in the middle of
     another program. It also notifies you when you receive a new
     message.¶

NP        ▌After being loaded, pressing <ALT-2> pops up a small window
     over your o╒══════════ cc:Mail MESSENGER ═══════════╗window
     you can rea║                                         ║cc:Mail
     features ar║ ▌Read inbox messages │ Prepare new message ║when
     moving an I║                                         ║know
     the name of╚═════════════════════════════════════════╝o
     select from█  ← → and ENTER to select, Esc to clear  █

-PD  **** INSERT CCM0101.PCX HERE¶

F1   Figudre 1.1 shows the Messenger window pop-up menu.¶

HE   (e)Notify¶
Pg4 Li21 Co6     {}              ?                    CCM01.DOC
```

Figure 1.1   The Messenger window pop-up menu.

Message
Pop-Up
Window

Notify

When first run, the Notify program checks your Inbox for any new messages. It continues to check your mailbox at predetermined intervals while you use other programs. When it detects a new message, it sounds a tone and displays a small window on the screen. You can also press Alt-2 at any time to have Notify check your mailbox and provide the display shown in Figure 1.2. To read any messages, however, you must exit your current program and run Mail, the main cc:Mail program.

Snapshot

Like Messenger and Notify, the Snapshot program must also be loaded before you can use another program. Once in another program, you use Snapshot to capture an image of the screen and save it to a file. That file can then be attached to a message as a graphic item, which enables the recipient to view the same screen you viewed when you captured the Snapshot image.

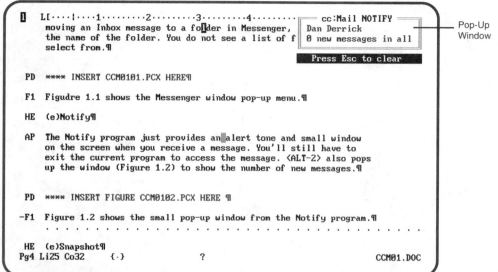

Pop-Up Window

Figure 1.2   The Notify pop-up window.

Overview of cc:Mail

This book covers both the DOS and Windows versions of cc:Mail. Both can be used to access the same mailboxes in a post office, and both share the same concepts of creating and accessing mail and managing folders and mailing lists. However, each program has a different method of execution.

Chapters 2 through 7 discuss the DOS version of cc:Mail but also include distinguishing information about the Windows version. The remaining chapters cover the Administrator program and other cc:Mail programs such as Gateway and Fax, which are designed to work under a variety of DOS-based programs.

DOS

This book is based on cc:Mail version 3.2. This version includes Notify, Messenger, and Snapshot and can run on any system. To produce graphics images, however, you need a graphics or Hercules-compatible display.

Menu Choices

All menus are presented as boxes appearing in the middle of the screen. The menu choices may vary depending on the actions available at that time. For example, Figure 1.3 shows two versions of the Main menu that differ owing to the presence or absence of messages in the Inbox.

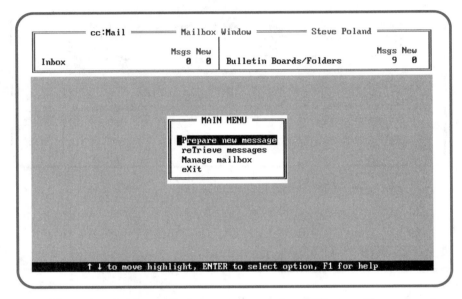

Figure 1.3   Menu choices may vary depending on the current conditions.

Menu choices can be selected in one of two ways. You can use the Arrow keys to move among menu items and then press Enter to choose the highlighted item. Or you can make your choice immediately by pressing the letter that corresponds to the brightly lit capital letter in each menu choice.

For example, the Address menu contains the choice eNd addressing. To select that choice, you move the highlight bar to that line and press Enter. Or you can just press N to perform the action immediately.

Most menus provide an option to return to the Main menu. The Esc key can also be used to exit the current process. If, by exiting, you will leave a task unfinished, cc:Mail asks you to confirm your choice to abandon that task.

Finding Help with the F1 Key

Many help screens are available when you press the F1 key. To find out more about a specific menu choice, move the highlight to that choice and press the F1 key. In many cases, the information presented will remain on the screen after you leave the Help window. To remove the Help window, press the Esc key.

Using a Mouse

The DOS version of cc:Mail does not use a mouse without special software. You must load software that translates the mouse actions into Arrow key movements before starting cc:Mail. For example, when you move the mouse up, the special software interprets this movement as a series of Up Arrow keystrokes. Likewise, pressing the button is like pressing Enter. This software may or may not have been supplied with your mouse. Without this software, mouse movements have no effect in the DOS version of cc:Mail.

9

Windows users can use a mouse with the standard movements, which are described in this book as follows:

Click	Quickly press and release the left mouse button.
Right-click	Quickly press and release the right mouse button.
Double-click	Quickly press the left mouse button twice.
Point	Move the mouse until the pointer rests on a specific area of the screen.
Drag	Press and hold the left button, then move the mouse to another location.

Windows

This book is based on cc:Mail version 1.1 for Windows. This program runs only under Microsoft Windows version 3.0 or later.

Using Icons

cc:Mail for Windows follows the Windows conventions for icons and pull-down menus. Menu choices can be accessed with the keyboard, but, as with all Windows applications, use of a mouse is preferable. The choices available from the Main window, shown in Figure 1.4, require fewer menu selections to perform cc:Mail functions than in the DOS-based version.

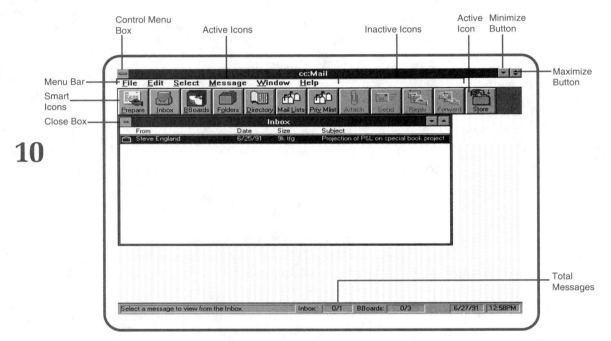

Figure 1.4   The opening screen for cc:Mail for Windows.

Multiple Windows

A cc:Mail session may contain a number of windows. Each item, highlighted in its own window, can be brought forward by clicking on that window. When you select a message from the Inbox list, it becomes a separate window. Once you finish with a message, you are returned to the next highest level.

As in all Windows applications, cc:Mail can be minimized into an icon and called back to full size by double-clicking this same cc:Mail icon. Once cc:Mail for Windows has been minimized, it can still check your mailbox at preset intervals. If new mail has arrived, the icon flashes or a message box pops up and a tone sounds, all based on the settings under File Options Notify.

Post Offices

The cc:Mail post office is the hub of the e-mail system. The system administrator establishes the name of the post office and other default settings while installing a copy of cc:Mail on the network. The administrator also decides which drive and subdirectories will contain the post office and cc:Mail programs.

Once the program is installed, the administrator creates and maintains all the mailboxes in the post office. Only the administrator (or anyone who knows the administrator's password) can change the post office name, add people or aliases to the mailing list, set up bulletin boards, and create public mailing lists, which are available to anyone using the post office.

11

Questions for Your Administrator

Because the system administrator decides these names and locations, it's a good idea to know how the administrator has designed the system. You may not need to know this information if you have a menu choice on your computer such as cc:Mail. In this case, you can just select the menu choice and begin running cc:Mail immediately. But, even with this option, you still need to know how your cc:Mail system is designed if you want to access your mailbox from any other system attached to the network.

Where Is Your cc:Mail Program?

The cc:Mail system consists of three parts: the user programs, the administrator's programs, and the actual data files. In most cases, all three of these elements are on the host system.

From the user's perspective, the host system and data files look like drives on your system. Before starting cc:Mail, you'll need to know which drive it's located on and which subdirectory contains the Mail program. Then, from the DOS prompt, you'll type a drive letter, change to the subdirectory, and start the program by typing `MAIL`.

What Is Your Address?

When the post office is first created, the administrator types in all the names. These become the mailbox addresses. You can access the post office only if you know the exact name that was typed for your mailbox. If your name is Rachael Daniels and your mailbox name was entered as Rachel Daniels, you'll never get to the first screen of cc:Mail by typing your correct name.

Where Are Your Data Files?

12

The data files are located in a subdirectory that functions as the post office. When starting cc:Mail, you'll have to tell the program where the post office is located, which may mean including a drive letter and a subdirectory name.

Starting a cc:Mail Session

You can start the cc:Mail program either by answering each of several questions or by providing all the answers at once. The first set of Quick Steps shows you how to start cc:Mail by answering each question. Once you know how to start cc:Mail in this manner, you may want to learn to use the quick way, which is outlined in the next series of Quick Steps.

The First Time

If you do not have the answers to the questions for your system administrator, you'll have to get them before you can continue. Write the answers in this space for future reference. You'll enter a special word in the password blank after you first sign on. This form is also reproduced on the inside back cover.

Question	Yours	Example
cc:Mail program drive:	_____	M:
cc:Mail subdirectory:	_____	\CCMAIL
Your address:	_____	Steve England
Drive and directory for the post office:	_____	M:\CCDATA
Password:	_____	ICE CREAM

Caution: Don't write your password down in the blank yet. Refer to the next section, "Your Password," for additional information before writing something in that blank.

Your Password

The need to use passwords depends on the size of your company and the need for security. Some system administrators require a password of at least eight characters that must be changed every 30 days. Other administrators dispense with passwords entirely. In this case, you just enter your name to start cc:Mail. The middle range might be a four-character password that you change only when you want.

The need for a unique password may become evident only after someone has signed on under your name, read your mail, and sent a less-than-helpful message to the president of the company (under your name, remember?). Here are some strategies for creating and remembering your password:

▶ Don't write the password down! If you write the password in the blank above, your mail is only as secure as where you leave this book. Instead, write a reminder to yourself about the password. If you use your mother's birthday, just write MOM in the blank. Or MOM might mean your mother's maiden name. Or MOM might mean the maiden name of you or your wife. This word just serves as the trigger.

► Passwords not to use: Your first name, nickname, initials, children's name, pet's name, birth date, or phone extension; the last four digits of your social security number; or ASDF, QWER, JKL:, or any quick string of keys on the keyboard.

► Password ideas: Your mother's maiden name, birth date, city of birth; a child's middle name, birth date, or favorite sport; a word from your favorite song, book, or movie; a city you once lived in; a company you once worked for; the date when something important happened, like the first day of summer camp (not your wedding anniversary); or, for even more security, a combination of two unrelated words, like paper-grass.

► If you do forget your password, the system administrator can create a new password without knowing the old one. The system administrator has access to all your messages on the network when he or she makes the change. Once you change it again, only you will have access to your mailbox.

14

 Starting the cc:Mail program

1. Change to the drive and subdirectory containing the Mail program.	The system prompt changes to that drive and directory.
2. Type **MAIL** and press Enter.	This starts a series of questions. The first is Post office address:. It may not appear, depending on how the cc:Mail system has been installed. If so, skip to step 4.
3. Type the post office address and press Enter.	The next prompt appears as Name:.
4. Type your exact name as used in your mailbox and press Enter.	The password prompt appears.
5. Type your new or existing password.	The first cc:Mail Main menu screen appears. □

Your first session might look like this:

```
C:\>M:
M:\>CD CCMAIL
M:\CCMAIL>MAIL
Post office address: M:\CCDATA
Name: Steve England
Enter new cc:Mail password: ŸŸŸŸŸŸŸ
```

You would then see the opening screen. You may not be prompted for the post office address. If your system administrator has copied both the data files and program files to the same directory, or if your data files are located in M:\ or M:\ccDate, the Mail program will find the post office immediately and prompt for your name and password.

 Caution: You must have rights to read, write, create and delete files in your current directory when you run mail.

15

The first time you use cc:Mail, you are prompted for a new password. This password can be changed later in cc:Mail. Whether or not you must enter a password, its length and the frequency with which it must be changed is determined by the system administrator. Notice that the password may or may not appear on your screen as you type it, depending on how the administrator configured the system.

 How did you select your password?

I chose two completely unrelated words at random, separated by a random character.

I used an old MIS trick.

Checking for Mail

Unless you use the Messenger or Notify programs, you must run cc:Mail to see if you have mail in your Inbox. How frequently you check for messages will depend on the amount of mail you receive and the need for timely responses.

The number of keystrokes necessary to start cc:Mail may be a deterrent to frequent checking. To help make this process quicker, the Mail program can be started by including all the information on one line. A sample might be:

```
M:\CCMAIL>MAIL STEVE ENGLAND 9856 M:\CCDATA
```

The program must know your mailbox name, your password, and the post office directory. Typing all this on one line takes you immediately into cc:Mail. But there is an even quicker way. You can create a small batch file to make this process equivalent to typing your first name. Even if you don't know anything about batch files, you can still create one with a few Quick Steps. Before you begin, make sure you know your mailbox address and the post office location. If you have started cc:Mail successfully, you already know these.

Remember, you don't need to use this method to access cc:Mail. You may want to come back to this later after you have tired of typing in all the information necessary to start cc:Mail. Make sure you are in your root directory before you start these Quick Steps. The system prompt should be `C:\>`.

 Creating a quick start for cc:Mail

1. Type the following, substituting your name for YOURNAME:
   COPY CON:YOURNAME.BAT
   Press Enter.

   The DOS prompt disappears.

2. Type the drive letter containing the cc:Mail program followed by a colon. Press Enter.

   The cursor moves to the next line.

3. Type the following, substituting a different subdirectory name if necessary:
   CD \CCMAIL
   Press Enter.

   The cursor moves to the next line.

4. Type the following, substituting your name for JOHN DOE and your post office address for M:\CCDATA:

   The cursor moves to the next line.

```
MAIL JOHN DOE %1 M:\CCDATA
```
Press Enter.

5. Press F6.   DOS responds with
                                                      1 File(s) copied.

6. To test this batch file type   The cc:Mail Main menu
   your first name and password.   appears.   □

You used the **%1** in place of the password. The batch file substitutes the word you enter after your first name when it starts the Mail program. This provides a quick way to start cc:Mail and still protect your password.

You can also replace the **%1** with your actual password. Then you need only type your name to get into cc:Mail. Remember, however, that this leaves your mailbox open to anyone who types your first name on your system.

Once you get this smoothed out (it may take a few tries), you can access your mailbox just by typing your name and password. If you want to know immediately when you have incoming mail, read Chapter 7, "Special Features and Programs."

17

 How frequently do you check your mail?

When I'm in my office, every few minutes.

At least four times a day, more often when necessary.

Several times daily.

Other Parameters

The cc:Mail command line can also accept several other parameters (words) on the same line. These parameters allow you to set paths for archive and DOS files automatically, change the order of your Inbox messages, suspend cc:Mail to return to DOS, and specify printer, monitor, and mouse settings. For more information on these parameters, ask your system administrator, who can refer to the appropriate section in the cc:Mail *User Reference Manual*.

Ending a Session

Once you have completed your session, you will need to exit the program. If this is your first time in cc:Mail, you can practice starting and ending the program without venturing any further if you like. Chapter 2 discusses how to read mail in your Inbox. Chapter 3 covers the basics of sending mail. For now, you've just learned how to open the door. Now you need to know how to close it. Next time in, you can wander around to see what is there.

Q **Exiting cc:Mail**

1. From the Main menu, move the highlight bar to eXit cc:mail and press Enter, or just press X.	You return to the DOS prompt immediately.

□

18

From any location in the cc:Mail menu system, you can press Esc until you reach this top menu. Once there, you must press X or highlight eXit cc:mail and press Enter. If it weren't for this feature, you could accidentally press Esc too many times and leave cc:Mail unintentionally.

For Windows Users

The cc:Mail for Windows program can be installed on the Windows Program Manager as an icon. You still need to know the same information from your system administrator. If you do not have a cc:Mail icon, contact your system administrator.

You start cc:Mail by double-clicking on the cc:Mail icon, usually including the words cc:Mail. Use the mouse to move the arrow to that icon and press the left mouse button twice quickly. The first time you use the program, you will be prompted for your name and the location of the post office. After the first session, you'll only have to supply the password. Figure 1.5 shows the dialog box after completing the password. Notice that the password does not appear as you type it.

You finish using cc:Mail as you do with all Windows programs. You double-click on the Control menu box in the extreme upper left corner. If you single-click, you can then click on the Close menu choice. From the keyboard, Alt-F4 will also end the Windows session.

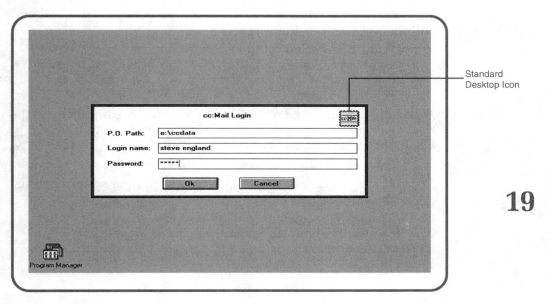

Standard Desktop Icon

19

Figure 1.5   The cc:Mail Dialog Box.

You may find it much more convenient to start cc:Mail and then minimize the program by clicking on the mininimize box (see Figure 1.4). You can then double-click on that icon at any time to continue your cc:Mail session.

> **Caution:** Remember that minimizing the cc:Mail program leaves your mailbox open to anyone with access to your computer. Any user can just click on the icon and begin reading your mail.

Remember that with cc:Mail active, it monitors your mailbox. Depending on your selections in File Options Notify, the program can check your mailbox at specific intervals for mail and notify you when new mail has been received.

What You Have Learned

▶ Electronic mail (e-mail) is a way to communicate with computers. You can send and receive text and graphic messages, which are addressed to mailboxes. You can also attach DOS files to messages.

▶ cc:Mail is installed on the network host computer by the system administrator. You must know where the cc:Mail files are located and how your name is used in the post office before you can start a session.

▶ Menu actions can be initiated by moving the highlight to the selection and pressing Enter or by typing the capitalized letter in that menu selection.

▶ The F1 key brings up a help screen for each menu selection.

▶ You can create a small batch file to save time when starting cc:Mail.

▶ Although Windows users start and end cc:Mail like other Windows programs, they still must know their post office location and mailbox name to complete the dialog box the first time.

Getting Mail

In This Chapter

► *Reading single-item messages*
► *Reading multi-item messages*
► *Selecting multiple messages*
► *Reading bulletin board messages*
► *Searching for messages*

Just like you have to check your mailbox at home, you have to remember to run cc:Mail on a regular basis to read messages others have sent. This chapter covers the process of reading your mail. You won't make any changes to a message as you follow the Quick Steps. Later, in Chapter 4, you will learn how to reply, file, and delete messages.

Reading Mail

You can tell immediately after starting cc:Mail how many messages you have in your Inbox. The upper left corner of the screen shows both the total number of messages and the number of unread messages since you last used cc:Mail. If you do not have any messages in your Inbox, skip to Chapter 3. In that chapter you'll learn how to send messages. Once you receive replies, you can return to this chapter to practice reading those messages.

Figure 2.1 shows that the user has seven messages in the Inbox, six of which are new since the last time he or she signed on. If there had been no messages, the Read inbox messages choice would not have been displayed and the Main menu would have had only four choices.

22

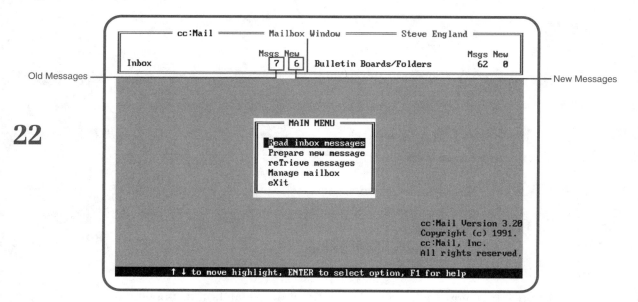

Old Messages — — New Messages

Figure 2.1   The Main menu with several messages available in the Inbox.

You can read messages through two menu choices. The most immediate and easiest is to select Read inbox messages. The second method, reTrieve messages, is covered in Chapter 5, "Managing Your Mailbox." This section will use that first choice because it is the quickest way to read your messages.

Reading a Message in the Inbox

1. From the Main menu, select Read inbox messages.

The Inbox list of messages appears.

2. Use the Up and Down Arrow keys to highlight the message you want to read. Use PgUp and PgDn to move through long lists. Press Enter when the highlight is on the message you want to read.

If the message contains just one item of text, you'll see the message immediately. If it contains more, you'll see an additional menu to select each item to view. ☐

All commands include a highlighted letter in the menu. You can always press that letter to save keystrokes. In the Read inbox messages menu choice, the letter R is highlighted and capitalized. You save a few keystrokes by pressing the letter choice for that menu selection.

After selecting Read inbox messages, cc:Mail displays the message titles in your Inbox. Figure 2.2 shows a sample list.

23

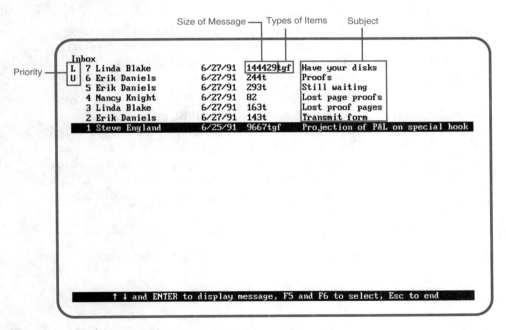

Figure 2.2   A sample Inbox message list.

This screen shows the message priority level, the message number, the sender, the date the message was sent, the total number of bytes used by the message, the types of items contained in the message, and the subject of the message. Lines in bold or a brighter color indicate messages that have not yet been read. After you have read the message, the line will be displayed in the normal color.

The sender sets the priority level when the message is first addressed. If that first column does not display a letter, the priority level is N for Normal. Low priority messages use an L. Higher priority messages use a U for Urgent. The sender sets these levels to get the reader's attention. What may be Normal priority for one person could be Urgent for someone else.

The second and third columns contain the sender's name and the date the message was originally sent. The messages are listed in the order received, with the most recent messages first. The fourth column shows the size of the message and, next to this figure, the types of message items. (The specific types of items are covered later in this chapter.) The last column indicates the message's subject, which the sender enters when writing the message.

All of these columns can help you decide which messages to read first. Some users select messages by the oldest date first and deal with the mail in chronological order. Others select messages by the level of urgency, and still others pick and choose based on the sender's name and subject.

Messages can remain in the Inbox even after you have read them. Like the inbox on your desk, you can sift through the messages and leave them in the Inbox. But a more efficient method is to read and deal with each message immediately. In some cases, you may move a message to a folder for further action. At least you will know that you have read the message, and you can deal with the contents of that folder later. (Folders are covered in Chapter 4, "Dealing with Each Message.")

24

 Do you have a method for dealing with your Inbox messages? If yes, what is it?

Do it now.

Basically the same way I deal with mail. I use the FAT system (File, Act, Trash).

Single-Item Messages

If the Inbox line includes a t after the size of the message, then the message in question contains only text. To read that message, you point to the message and press Enter. The message will immediately appear on the screen, as in the sample shown in Figure 2.3. The top line shows the message number on the list, the sender, the date and time the message was sent, and the total size of the message. The second and third lines show the recipient(s) of the message and the subject.

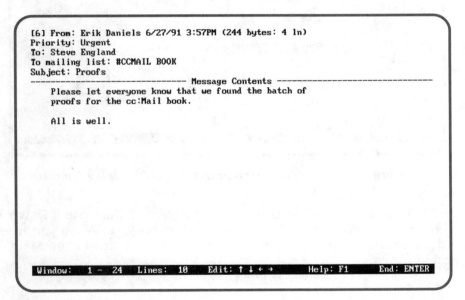

```
[6] From: Erik Daniels 6/27/91 3:57PM (244 bytes: 4 ln)
Priority: Urgent
To: Steve England
To mailing list: #CCMAIL BOOK
Subject: Proofs
------------------------------ Message Contents ------------------------------
   Please let everyone know that we found the batch of
   proofs for the cc:Mail book.

   All is well.




  Window:    1 - 24   Lines:  10    Edit: ↑ ↓ ← →       Help: F1      End: ENTER
```

Figure 2.3   A sample text message.

25

> **Tip:** Since the same message can be sent to more than one person, the To: line will also list others who received this same message.

Pressing Enter after a message is displayed produces the menu shown in Figure 2.4, which allows you to direct the message in a number of ways. These topics are covered in Chapter 4, "Dealing with Each Message." To continue reading mail, press Enter. Since the highlight is on display Next message, you are returned to the Inbox message list.

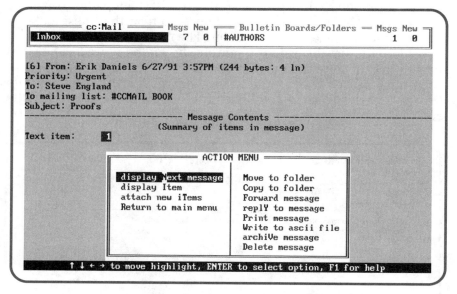

Figure 2.4   The Action menu presented after reading a message.

You can then move to another message with the Up and Down Arrow keys and press Enter to read another message. When you are done reading messages, you can press Esc to return to the Main menu.

Selecting and Reading Multiple Messages

If you have a lot of messages to read and handle, you can select them at the same time on the Inbox list. The Action menu then allows you to perform one action on all the files you've selected. In the following example you'll select messages from the Inbox list to read in sequence. When you finish dealing with one message, you'll go immediately to the next message on this list.

Marking and Unmarking Messages in the Inbox List

1. Move the highlight to each specific message you want to read and press F5.

   A small arrow appears on the left edge of the screen.

2. To mark a block of messages, move to the first message and press F5.

   This marks that message.

3. Move to the last message in the list and press F6.

   Every message between the first and last marks will now be marked with an arrow.

4. To unmark messages, press F5 to turn off the mark, then use Esc to unmark all the messages and start over.

   If you press Esc again, you return to the Main menu.

5. Once you have marked all the messages, press Enter.

   The Action menu appears. □

27

The bottom of the Inbox list reminds you that the F5 and F6 keys are used in this selection process. However, the F6 key does not unmark a block. You can use the Esc key, but it unmarks all the messages in the list. Figure 2.5 shows two marked messages.

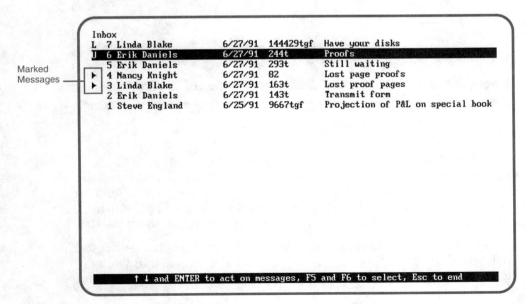

Figure 2.5   Two messages marked with the F5 key.

> **Tip:** If you want to read most, but not all, of the messages in the list, mark the first line with F5. Move to the last line and press F6. Then unmark the few you don't want to read with the F5 key.

Now when you press Enter, you'll see the Action menu shown in Figure 2.6. The number of messages selected is in the upper left part of the screen. This Action menu provides seven ways to handle the marked messages. For now, you just want to read them, so select `display All messages`.

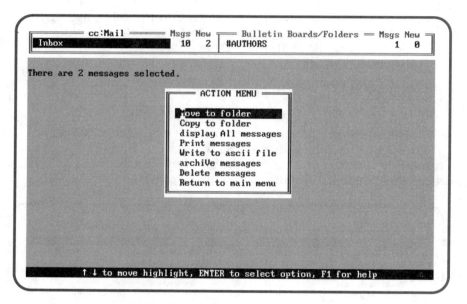

Figure 2.6   The Action menu.

The first message will be displayed on the screen as before. After you press Enter to finish reading that message, you'll see the larger Action menu originally shown in Figure 2.4. The difference occurs when you select `display Next message`. Instead of returning to the Inbox list, you'll see the next message you selected on the list.

Once you have finished reading all the messages in the selected list, you'll see the Action menu again. cc:Mail assumes that you may want to perform another action on these selected messages. If you want to return to the Inbox list, use Esc. The messages will still be marked. If you return to the Main menu and then return to the Inbox list, the messages will no longer be marked.

> **Caution:** If you press Enter after reading the last message and then press Enter again accidentally at the Action menu, you will have moved those marked messages to a folder. You can still read and use them but they will no longer be in your Inbox. Chapter 4 explains how to retrieve a message from a folder.

Multi-Item Messages

29

Although many messages are just short notes from one person to another, cc:Mail messages can also include graphics, DOS files, and faxes. The Inbox item list indicates the types of items next to the figure for the size of the message. These items are designated by letters, as listed in Table 2.1.

Table 2.1   The Types of Message Items

Letter	Contents
t	Text item created in cc:Mail
g	Graphics item created in cc:Mail graphic editor or captured with the cc:Mail Snapshot program
f	Any DOS file
x	A fax item

Text

Any message you type using the cc:Mail editor is a text item, as is any information from a folder or bulletin board that you include in your message. All these text items are useable only in cc:Mail. The actual files on the disk are totally scrambled and are not readable by anyone except the sender, recipient, and system administrator.

One way to expand access to your messages is to write text items to an ASCII file from the Action menu. Once the item has been copied to this file on the computer's disk, it can be used in word processing software by anyone with access to the file.

Text messages can also be printed from the Action menu. If your designated printer is local (next to you), you alone will get the printed page. If you use a network printer, the message can be read by anyone else with access to that printer.

Graphics

Graphic items are displayed only if you have a graphic screen. If your monitor shows only text, graphic items are not displayed on your message item list. Check with your system administrator if you are not sure what kind of screen you have.

Like other message items, graphic images can be printed to a graphic printer, copied or moved to a folder or bulletin board, or forwarded to another address. Although a graphic image cannot be copied to a DOS file from the Action menu, it can be "extracted" from the message using Snapshot and then saved as a graphics file. (See Chapter 7, "Special Features and Programs.")

You can create graphic images in two ways with cc:Mail. You can either use the Graphic Editor program to create images such as maps or quick sketches or you can capture screen images from other programs with the Snapshot program. (See Chapter 7 for more on these programs.) For example, if you wanted to show someone a screen-sized section of a spreadsheet, you could capture that section and then attach it to a message. You can use the Graphic Editor to make notes on that screen shot of the spreadsheet image. Both the Graphic Editor and Snapshot images are limited in size to one screen.

 What kind of graphic images do you get and send?

Sales territories, screen shots.

Various types, usually in the form of attached application files.

GIF and PCX files and PageMaker documents.

DOS Files

A DOS file can be attached to a message as an item. Any file listing in a directory, including data and program files, can be used as part of a message item. The recipient can then use the DOS file after it has been copied to his or her disk. Unless you erase the item or delete the message, that file remains attached to the message.

For example, if you want to send a spreadsheet you have created with Lotus 1-2-3 as part of a message, you first save that spreadsheet file to disk. Then you attach that file to a cc:Mail message as a DOS file. Once the recipient reads your message, he or she can copy that file from the message back to a disk, from which the original spreadsheet can be loaded and used with a local copy of Lotus 1-2-3.

Facsimile

31

Fax images can be attached to messages just like DOS files. The cc:Mail Fax and Gateway programs allow you to send any message to a designated facsimile machine. If a computer has been established with a phone number and special fax board, you can also view any fax message sent to that computer. In short, with these programs you can use the cc:Mail system to communicate with fax machines as easily as with computers.

 How much do you use the Fax program?

I use it frequently to get responses to folks who don't have electronic mail. I can cut and paste and send!

The following Quick Steps show you how to read messages with these different types of items attached.

 Viewing Multi-item messages

1. Select a multi-item message indicated by f, g, or x.	The Action menu appears with display Items highlighted.
2. Press Enter or I.	The message does not contain the To: /From: information at the top.

3. Press Enter when you have finished reading the message.

The Action menu returns.

4. To view the next readable item, press Enter.

If the next item is a file, the menu highlight will be on sKip to next item and you'll move to the next item number. If it is a text file, you'll see it on the screen.

5. Press Esc any time to return to the Inbox list.

Once you have worked your way through all the items, you'll return to the Inbox list or the next selected message. □

32

When you select a message in the Inbox list with more than one item attached (for example, a text and a graphic item), the Action menu screen appears as shown in Figure 2.7. This Action menu is the same menu you see after viewing a message with just a text file. Since the highlight starts on display Items, you can press Enter or I to see the first item.

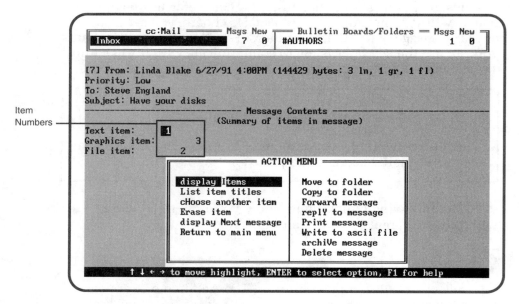

Item Numbers

Figure 2.7   The Action menu shown when a multi-item message has been selected.

The message shown in Figure 2.8 does not contain a message address at the top, just the actual text. That's because the pertinent information is displayed in the Action menu. After viewing that first item, you'll see a new top line highlighted on the Action menu, sKip to next item. Compare Figures 2.7 and 2.9 to note the new menu choices and the movement of the item number highlight in the Action menu.

If you press Enter, the item number highlight moves to the next item number containing a text item. Since, in the current example, this is an attached DOS file, cc:Mail assumes you cannot read it as a text message. Therefore, you need to use the cOpy file item to dos menu choice before you can use that DOS file. For more information about dealing with attached files, see Chapter 4.

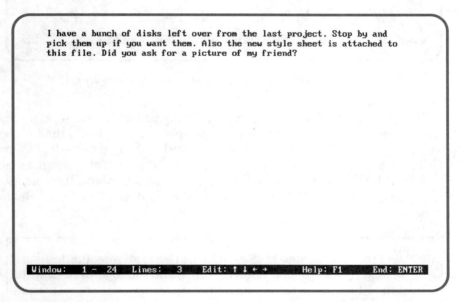

33

Figure 2.8   The different text message format in a multi-item message.

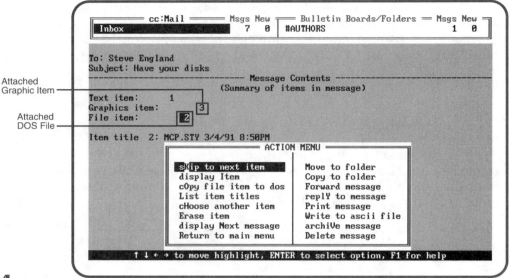

Attached Graphic Item —

Attached DOS File —

Figure 2.9   The different menu displayed for file items.

If you want to display the list of items, select the menu choice List item titles. This removes the Action menu and lists the items as shown in Figure 2.10. Use the Up and Down Arrows to move through this list and then press Enter to bring up that item as a message. Once you have examined all the text items, you'll return to the Inbox message list. From there you can continue to select messages to read.

> **Tip:** Remember that a DOS file is rarely readable as a text message. You'll have to copy the file to your disk and load the file into the same program the sender used to create the file.

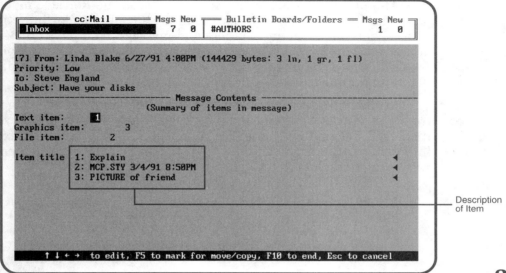

Figure 2.10   A multi-item message that is ready to be viewed by item numbers and titles.

Selecting Messages to Read

Your Inbox, folders, archive files, and bulletin boards can contain hundreds of messages. To retrieve only the messages you want to work with or view, you use the Retrieve menu. The search portion of this menu allows you to select a specific group of messages based on the person sending the message, a keyword phrase, the date, the priority level, and more. You can use the selection process several times to narrow the search. After each selection, cc:Mail shows the number of selected messages.

Once you have narrowed down the list, you can scan message headings to select individual messages to view or perform some other action. You'll be prompted after each message just as you are when reading multiple messages from your Inbox.

The number of messages first available in the Retrieve menu depends on the number of active users, the number of bulletin boards, and the number of folders and messages you have created and saved. There can easily be hundreds of messages to sort through. For this reason, you are more likely to select a bulletin board or folder before searching for messages.

In all, there are several ways to narrow the number of messages from the Retrieve menu, and not all of these methods will be displayed. Depending on the area you want to search (folder, Inbox, bulletin board, or archive file), you'll encounter some or all of these search methods:

> **search for msg nUmbers** You can narrow the search for messages by limiting the selection to specific message numbers or a range of numbers. For example, to select messages 3, 4, 10, 11, 12 and 13, you could use 3, 4, 10-13. This search method is available only within a specific bulletin board or folder.
>
> **search by Person** When you select this search method, the cc:Mail directory appears. You can then select a name to be searched in the To: or From: lines of each message.
>
> **search by Keyword phrase** Once you type a keyword or phrase up to 30 characters long, cc:Mail searches the subject line and the item titles for that phrase.
>
> **search by Calendar date** The calendar date search looks at the message date on or after a date you provide and on or before a date you provide. For example, if you specify a date in the on or after prompt and leave the on or before prompt blank, you will select all messages created on or after that date.
>
> **search by priority Level** Messages can be assigned priority levels of Urgent, Normal, and Low. Selecting one level limits the messages to that specific priority level. Most messages are sent as Normal priority.

 Caution: If you narrow down the selections too much, you'll run out of messages to read and have to start over.

What method do you use to search for messages?

I archive messages by month and use cc:Mail's text search capabilities.

I maintain multiple folders that usually relate to the subject of the conversation.

The next section displays some of the search methods for a bulletin board. Remember that these methods also work on your Inbox, folders, and archive files.

Reading Bulletin Boards

Ordinary messages are sent from one individual to another or to a specific group of people. Other than the system administrator, no one else can read those messages. Bulletin board messages are different. They are public to all users, and therefore anyone can read and respond to them. Only the system administrator and the sender can delete a message from the board.

 Caution: Since everyone can read messages, consider carefully what you post on the bulletin board for everyone to see.

Because a bulletin board may contain many messages, you may want to search for specific messages by using the search criteria. The following Quick Steps show you how to select and then search for messages from a bulletin board.

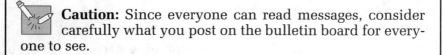 **Selecting Messages from a Bulletin Board**

1. From the Main menu, select `reTrieve messages`.

   The Action menu appears with the highlight on `retrieve from bboard/ Folder`.

2. Press Enter or F.

A list of bulletin boards and your folders appears.

3. Select a specific bulletin board name beginning with the # character.

That board name appears on the screen as well as the number of messages currently selected.

4. Select search by Calendar date.

The on or after date prompt appears.

5. Enter a date as mm/dd/yy. The date format is month/day/year, as in 08/26/91. The date must include the / character.

The on or before date prompt appears.

6. To include all messages up to today's date, press Enter.

The new number of messages selected appears along with the Retrieve menu.

7. Select scan message Headings.

The list of messages appears.

8. Use F5 to mark messages and then press Enter.

The Action menu appears.

9. Select display All messages.

This begins the read sequence and the Action menu sequence.

10. Select Return to main menu. You can also use ESC at any time to start over.

The Main menu appears.

□

Figure 2.11 shows the retrieve from bboard/Folder choice on the Retrieve menu. If you make this selection immediately by pressing Enter or F, you can then select a specific bulletin board or folder to look in, as shown in Figure 2.12. The Arrow keys move the highlighted line down the list of bulletin boards (noted by # before the name) and folders. The list will scroll up if there are more boards or folders. Press Enter to select that board or folder. (Folders will be covered in Chapter 4, "Dealing with Each Message.")

Once you select a bulletin board, you can use additional search categories to reduce the number of messages you have to view from that specific bulletin board or folder. Whether you first select a board or just want to scan the entire message base, the selection process on the Retrieve menu is the same.

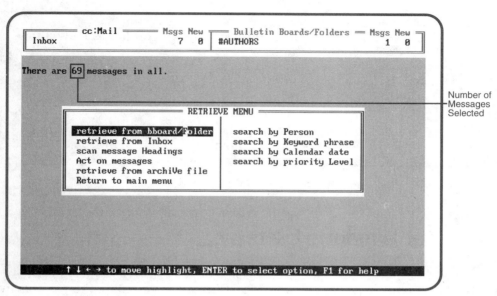

Figure 2.11   The Retrieve menu.

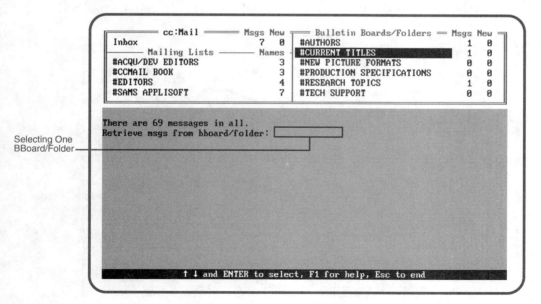

Figure 2.12   A sample list of bulletin boards to select.

What types of bulletin boards do you have? How much do you use them?

We use our bulletin boards for company news, stock news, faxable copies of all our brochures, news for the field, etc.

We don't use bulletin boards that much, since we've had a bulletin board system implemented on our mainframe.

For Windows Users

40

To read mail with cc:Mail for Windows, you start the session by pointing with the mouse and double-clicking on your Mail icon. Once the program starts, cc:Mail immediately provides the Inbox list of messages, as shown in Figure 2.13.

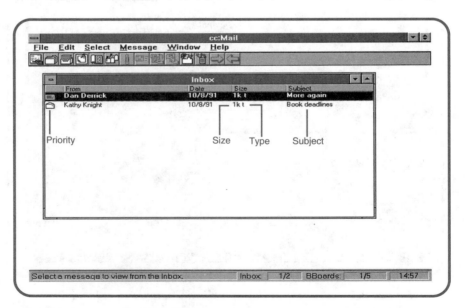

Figure 2.13   The opening screen for cc:Mail for Windows.

> **Caution:** cc:Mail contains dozens of icons that can be used in the Windows Program Manager. The standard icon is a stamp with the words cc:Mail. If someone else has installed cc:Mail, they may have selected a different icon and description for the cc:Mail program.

To read a message in the Inbox, double-click on that message line. If the message contains only one text message, a screen similar to Figure 2.14 is displayed. To return to the Inbox list without making any changes to this message, double-click on the small square with a hyphen (known as the *Close box*) on the upper left edge of the menu bar. This leaves the message in the Inbox. In most cases, you would perform some action on the message by pointing to one of the icons at the top of the screen. Chapter 4 covers the process of responding to and saving messages.

41

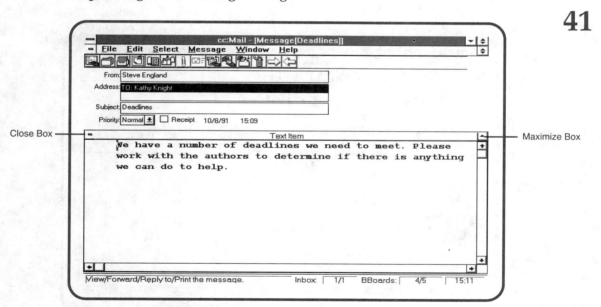

Figure 2.14   A message just selected from the Inbox list.

To select several messages to read sequentially, press the Ctrl key and then click on each message to read. On the last message you select, double-click while holding down the Ctrl key. cc:Mail opens a window for each message. After you double-click on the Close box, that window closes and the next message window appears.

To select a list of messages to read, use the Shift key. Select the first message, press the Shift key, and then select the message at the end of the list. All the messages in between will be highlighted. Each message will be opened in its own window.

If the message has more than one item attached, the message items will be displayed as separate icons, as in Figure 2.15. To view an item, just point to it and double-click. If the icon is a text item, the text will be displayed as a normal text message. If the item shows the DOS screen, it is a DOS file and must be copied to disk before it can be used. Attempting to view it will not damage the file, but the image won't mean anything. To close, click on the Close box in the upper left corner of the display window.

42

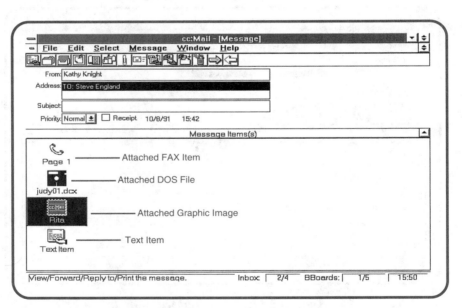

Figure 2.15   A multi-item message screen.

If you choose to view and fax graphic items attached to a message, it will appear after a short delay, during which cc:Mail translates the graphic image into a Windows format. Your screen will now look similar to the one shown in Figure 2.16. You can open up the viewing area by clicking on the small Up Arrow icon (known as the Maximize box) in the upper right corner of the viewing window. To close the window and return to the multi-item selection, click on the Close box in the upper left corner of the display window.

To read messages posted on bulletin boards, click on the BBoard icon at the top of the screen. You will then see a list of bulletin boards, as shown in Figure 2.17. To select a specific board to look at, simply double-click on that line. Once that board is active, the list of messages is presented and used just like the Inbox message list.

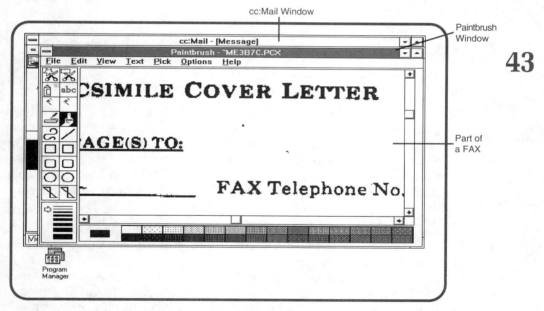

Figure 2.16   Paintbrush called up to show a FAX.

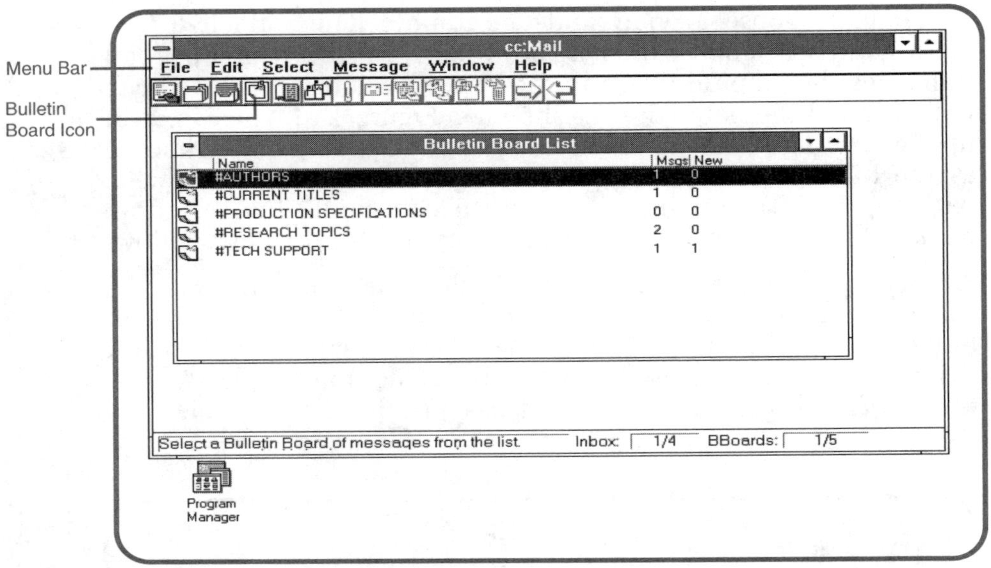

Menu Bar

Bulletin
Board Icon

Figure 2.17   A sample bulletin board list.

Any list of messages including the Inbox, Folders and Bulletin Boards can be searched for specific words or phrases. You can select the Search dialog box from the Edit menu or, if you have installed the Search icon (a flashlight) as a SmartIcon, you can just click on that SmartIcon. Once selected, the Search dialog box, shown in Figure 2.18, prompts for a word or phrase. The areas to be selected vary, depending on the source of the messages.

For example, searching for a specific word in the folder list can only be based on the title of the folder. But, once a folder has been opened, the search can include the From: and Subject: lines. An even more extensive search can include the message text as well. Once located, the item is highlighted. Just double-click on that line to open that message window. The Search dialog box remains on the screen and can be used to continue the search. Click the Done button to close the dialog box.

Tip: The ability to search entire messages for words or phrases is very powerful, but may take quite a while if there are a number of messages to search. Make sure the check box next to Messages is empty unless you really need to search each complete message for the word or phrase.

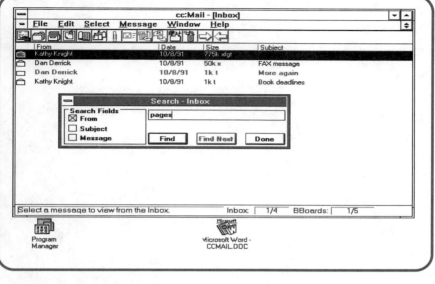

Figure 2.18   The Edit Search Dialog Box.

45

What You Have Learned

▶ You can read an individual message from the Inbox list by moving the highlight to the line and pressing Enter.

▶ Windows users double-click on a message line to bring up the message window.

▶ There are four types of items possible in each message: text, graphic, DOS files, and fax.

▶ Each item in a multi-item message can be individually selected.

▶ Messages can be located by message number, person, date, keyword, and priority.

▶ Bulletin boards are established by the system administrator and contain messages for everyone to read and use.

Chapter 3

Sending Mail

In This Chapter

- ► *Addressing messages*
- ► *Using the cc:Mail Editor*
- ► *Using another word processor*
- ► *Setting priority levels*
- ► *Requesting return receipt*

For an e-mail system to become an important communications channel within your organization, you must be able to send messages quickly and easily. cc:Mail allows you to send basic text messages in three steps: by selecting the address, by typing the text and attaching items, and then by sending the message.

Addressing

Messages can be sent to one or more individuals, to a predefined list of people, to a bulletin board, or to any combination of addresses. In all cases, when you send mail, you select the specific address from a list of available addresses.

These are the Quick Steps for addressing a message to an individual. Later in this chapter you'll learn how to type the text and send the message.

 Addressing a message

1. From the Main menu, select Prepare new message.

   The Address menu appears with Address to person highlighted.

2. Press Enter or A.

   The mailing list directory for individuals appears.

3. Use the Up and Down Arrows to highlight the name you want and then press Enter. Or you can begin typing the name. Once the highlight has moved to the name you want, press Enter.

   The name appears on the To: line of the address. The directory list remains on the screen.

4. Use Esc to finish.

   The Address menu appears with the highlight on eNd addressing.

5. Press Enter or N.

   The cursor moves to the Subject: line.

6. Type the contents for the Subject: line and press Enter.   □

The cursor moves to the message area of the screen. You are now ready to type your text message.

Caution: Do not press Esc on the Address menu. This abandons the complete address and subject line and returns you to the Main menu without warning.

48

To which do you send most of your mail: individuals, public lists, or private lists?

Most of my mail is distributed to individuals and private lists.

We use all three, but primarily private lists.

Using the Mail Directory

After selecting Prepare new message from the Main menu, you'll see the Address menu shown in Figure 3.1. You use this menu to fill in the To: (second) line of the message, which can only be completed with these selections. By picking names from an existing list, you can't mistype a name or send mail to someone who no longer has a mailbox in your post office.

49

```
From: Steve England 6/28/91 2:28PM
To:
Subject:
──────────────────────── Message Contents ────────────────────────
None




                    ════════ ADDRESS MENU ════════
           ┌──────────────────────────────────────────────┐
           │ Address to person        Copy to person      │
           │ address to Mailing list  copy to mailing List │
           │ address to bboard/Folder Blind copy to person │
           │ eNd addressing           set Priority level   │
           │ Return to main menu      reQuest receipt      │
           └──────────────────────────────────────────────┘




    ↑ ↓ ← → to move highlight, ENTER to select option, F1 for help
```

Figure 3.1   The Address menu.

The Address to person choice brings up a directory list similar to the one shown in Figure 3.2. This is an individual list with last names first. The Loc column shows the individual's type of mailbox, indicated by L for local and R for remote. The lowercase a shows that the name is an alias, a nickname for someone already on the list. For example, Nancy is an alias for Knight, Nancy. Selecting either of these two choices will address the message to Nancy Knight.

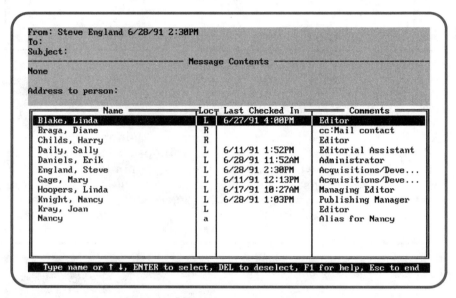

```
From: Steve England 6/28/91 2:30PM
To:
Subject:
------------------------------ Message Contents ------------------------------
None

Address to person:

======= Name =======  ┬Loc┬ Last Checked In ┬======= Comments =======
Blake, Linda           L   6/27/91 4:00PM     Editor
Braga, Diane           R                      cc:Mail contact
Childs, Harry          R                      Editor
Daily, Sally           L   6/11/91 1:52PM     Editorial Assistant
Daniels, Erik          L   6/28/91 11:52AM    Administrator
England, Steve         L   6/28/91 2:30PM     Acquisitions/Deve...
Gage, Mary             L   6/11/91 12:13PM    Acquisitions/Deve...
Hoopers, Linda         L   6/17/91 10:27AM    Managing Editor
Knight, Nancy          L   6/28/91 1:03PM     Publishing Manager
Kray, Joan             L                      Editor
Nancy                  a                      Alias for Nancy




═══════════════════════════════════════════════════════════════════════════════
  Type name or ↑ ↓, ENTER to select, DEL to deselect, F1 for help, Esc to end
```

Figure 3.2   The individual mailing directory.

All address directories provide two ways to select a name. One is to move the highlight bar to the name using the Up and Down Arrows and the PgUp and PgDn keys. Once the name you want is highlighted, press Enter. This copies that label to the To: line of the message.

Another approach, useful with long mailing directories, is just to begin typing the name. As you type each letter, the mailing directory will narrow the possible selections. As soon as the highlight is on the name you want, press Enter. If you continue to type a name that does not exist in the mailing directory, the program will beep and provide an error message stating that New names may not be entered. The warning window will clear in a few seconds, or you may clear it with the Esc key.

Figure 3.3 shows a single name on the To: line. The Subject: line has been completed and a short note entered.

If you want to send the message to several people, you continue to select names. Each name will be added to the list of people on the

To: line. When you are done adding names, you can press Esc or just press Enter again on the last name you selected. The Address menu appears. Once you have finished, select eNd addressing.

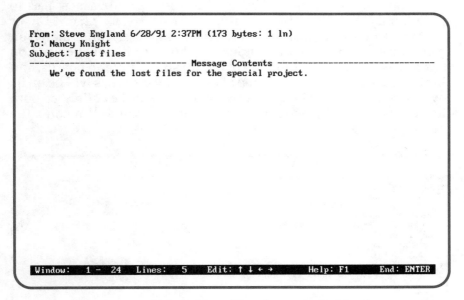

```
From: Steve England 6/28/91 2:37PM (173 bytes: 1 ln)
To: Nancy Knight
Subject: Lost files
------------------------------- Message Contents -------------------------------
    We've found the lost files for the special project.




















 Window:  1 - 24   Lines:   5    Edit: ↑ ↓ ← →        Help: F1      End: ENTER
```

Figure 3.3   A sample address line for an individual.

Tip: From the Main menu you can quickly address a message to one person by typing PA, typing the first few letters of his or her last name until that name is highlighted, and then pressing Enter three times.

Correcting the Address

If you need to delete an address before you select eNd addressing from the Address menu, return to that list and highlight that name again. Press the Del key, and the name disappears from the To: line. Use Esc to return to the Address menu.

Once you have begun typing the message, you can use F10 to move to the Send menu. When you select Address message, you return to the Address menu. You can then make any additions or deletions. After selecting eNd addressing, you can return to the text of the message with display Message on the Send menu.

51

Including Mailing Lists and Bulletin Boards

When sending messages to mailing lists and bulletin boards, you need to follow the same basic steps as when sending messages to individuals. You start by selecting address to Mailing list or address to bboard/Folder from the Address menu. From there you can proceed to narrow your choice of addresses if you choose. You can also select any combination of mailing lists, bulletin boards, and individuals to address. Each one of these address types will be on its own line, as shown in Figure 3.4. Should someone be addressed both individually and in a mailing list, he or she will still receive the message only once.

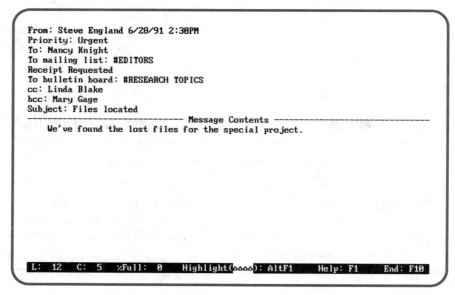

Figure 3.4   A sample address with multiple entries.

Multiple-entry addresses can be extremely useful. For example, if you have a message of general interest on a specific bulletin board topic but also want to make sure that several coworkers see the message, you can send the message to their individual mailboxes as well as to the selected bulletin board.

Copy To...

The Address menu also allows you to select Copy to person, copy to mailing List, and Blind copy to person. You make these menu choices and select the names from the mailing lists. Names selected for copy to... show on the address line of the recipient message as cc:. Names selected for Blind copy do not show on the original recipient's copy of the message.

> **Tip:** The notation cc: at the bottom of a letter used to stand for carbon copy. In our day of copy machines and electronic mail, it stands for courtesy copy.

Priority Level

You set the priority level of your message from the Address menu. The default level is Normal. On the Inbox message list, the priority level is indicated on the left edge of the list. Normal priority messages do not have any indication at all. Urgent or Low priority messages will have a U or L in that column.

You can also use the priority level to sort out messages with the Search feature. The need to change this level will depend on the number of messages that pass through the cc:Mail system and the conventions used in your post office. If everyone sets his or her priority level to Urgent, that setting will not have any meaning, and Low priority messages will consequently suggest junk mail.

If you decide that you need to change the priority level, select set Priority level from the Address menu. At the prompt, press U for Urgent, L for Low, or N for Normal. If you set the message for Urgent or Low, an additional line will appear in the address section showing that priority.

> **What kinds of messages do you use priority messages for?**
>
> Usually when I know the other person is waiting for the document or message that I'm sending.
>
> None. We use the Notify feature to notify users of all new mail each time they log in to the network.

Request Receipt

The Address menu has a menu choice for reQuest receipt. When you select this, the address section of the message adds the line Receipt Requested. The menu choice then changes to cancel receipt reQuest. Selecting this again will turn off the request.

When a user receives a message with Receipt Requested, he or she will experience a slight delay before seeing the text while cc:Mail generates a brief message back to you, the sender. (You will receive receipts only from people on the To: line, but not from those on the cc: or bcc: lines.) Your Inbox will then contain a message showing the time the message was read and the contents of the Subject: line.

> **Tip:** Make sure your Subject: line contains enough information to help you remember what the original message contained.

> **For what kinds of messages do you use a return receipt?**
>
> I rarely use it unless it's an urgent message that I want to be able to follow up on if I haven't received a return receipt in the expected time frame.
>
> Usually I use it for dated materials that I need to know were received by a certain time.

Entering Text

Many of the messages you send will consist only of text, which you will type with the cc:Mail Editor program. Editor contains some of the features found in standard word processing software. It also contains a feature unique to cc:Mail—the ability to highlight specific words or sections with different screen colors.

Although Editor can handle up to 20,000 characters, you may want to use your favorite word processing program to create messages longer than a page. For shorter messages and responses to other messages, however, Editor is quicker.

Once you have moved the cursor to the main part of the message screen, the bottom line of the screen provides information about cursor location in the text and about several function keys. Figure 3.5 shows a sample screen with the beginning of a message.

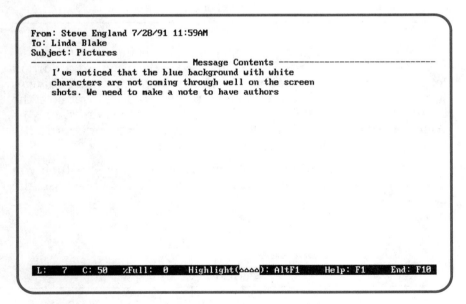

```
From: Steve England 7/28/91 11:59AM
To: Linda Blake
Subject: Pictures
------------------------------- Message Contents -------------------------------
    I've noticed that the blue background with white
    characters are not coming through well on the screen
    shots. We need to make a note to have authors




L:   7   C: 50   %Full:  0    Highlight(◦◦◦◦): AltF1      Help: F1      End: F10
```

Figure 3.5   A message typed with the Editor program.

To move within a document you use the Arrow keys. The Home key moves to the upper left corner of the screen. The End key moves to the last line of text on the screen. The PgUp and PgDn keys move the text 12 lines at a time. F3 moves to the beginning of a line of text. Pressing F3 again moves the cursor to the end. Table 3.1 shows all the cursor movement keys.

Table 3.1   Cursor Movement Keys

Key(s)	Movement
← →	One character left or right
↑ ↓	One line up or down
Home	To upper left corner of the screen
Ctrl-Home	To upper left corner of the text item
End	To last line on the screen
Ctrl-End	To last line of text item
PgUp	Up 12 lines
Ctrl-PgUp	Up 24 lines
PgDn	Down 12 lines
Ctrl-PgDn	Down 24 lines
Tab	One tab position to right
Shift-Tab	One tab position to left
F3	To end or beginning of line

When Editor is first activated the cursor is in *overstrike* mode, which means that the next character typed will overwrite the current letter. To shift to *insert* mode, press the Ins key. The cursor changes to a small block, and now any characters typed will be inserted at the current location. To delete a letter to the left of the cursor, use the Backspace key. To delete the letter on which the cursor is currently located, use the Del key.

When you have finished editing the message, press F10. If you press Enter the cursor will just move to the next line. Likewise, the Esc key will only place small arrows on the screen. Table 3.2 provides a summary of editing keys.

Table 3.2   Editing Keys

Key	Purpose
Ins	Toggles insert and overstrike mode
Del	Deletes character on the cursor
Backspace	Deletes character to left of cursor
Alt-F4	Deletes entire line cursor is on
F10	Finishes editing of document

The Editor program can also mark blocks, search and replace, and find a word or phrase. Using the F1 key while in Editor will display all the additional editing keys available. For more information about these features, consult your system administrator.

 What are some tips for using the Editor?

I love highlighting!

The most valuable tool I've found is the Alt-F9 text in. It allows me to use my word processor for large messages, then directly read them into the cc:Mail message.

Highlighting Text

57

One unique feature available in Editor is highlighting. You can emphasize text as you type or after it has been entered. Alt-F1 brings up the Highlighting menu shown in Figure 3.6. You use the Up and Down Arrows to cycle the background colors through eight different colors. The Right and Left Arrows cycle the foreground (letter) colors. The small box in the lower right corner represents the selected color combination. Press Enter to choose that as the current color combination. Use Esc to return to the colors you started with.

Once you have selected a new color scheme, all text and changes to text will appear in that combination, which is noted at the bottom of the screen.

You can change current text colors by using the F2 key. Place the cursor on the text you wish to change and then press F2. The text over the cursor changes and the cursor moves to the next character. Continue for all the text you want highlighted.

To set the color combination that exists at the current cursor position, press Alt-F1 and then Enter.

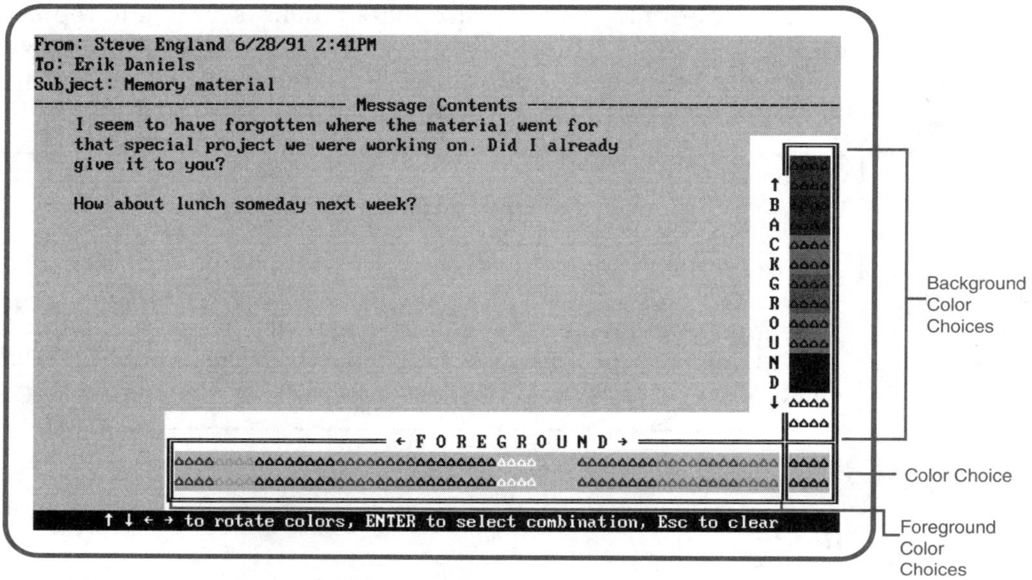

From: Steve England 6/28/91 2:41PM
To: Erik Daniels
Subject: Memory material
──────────────────── Message Contents ────────────────────
I seem to have forgotten where the material went for
that special project we were working on. Did I already
give it to you?

How about lunch someday next week?

Background
Color
Choices

↑ ← FOREGROUND → ↓

Color Choice

Foreground
Color
Choices

↑ ↓ ← → to rotate colors, ENTER to select combination, Esc to clear

Figure 3.6   The Highlight choices in Editor.

Caution: If you leave a color combination active when you finish a message, that combination carries over to the next message and the next cc:Mail session.

Your system administrator can set the default color combination, or, as noted, you can set the color to something you prefer. cc:Mail also translates any color highlighting between monochrome and color screens and back again. Messages passed between users with these different monitors still retain their color highlight settings. To change these settings permanently, see Chapter 5, "Managing Your Mailbox."

Using Another Word Processor

cc:Mail does not contain features some users consider essential, especially spell checking and "undo" delete. Those missing features, and the need to learn a whole new set of editing commands, may restrict the length of your text messages in cc:Mail. However, users can create messages in their usual word processor and save the file as an ASCII (text) file. This generic format can then be easily read by cc:Mail and other word processors.

The following Quick Steps show you how to use your favorite word processor to create longer text messages in cc:Mail. Chapter 7, "Special Features and Programs," shows you how to leave your word processing program active while creating cc:Mail text messages.

 Creating a text message to use in cc:Mail

1. Compose the message with your preferred word processing software. Save the file using a text or ASCII format and note exactly which drive and directory contain the file.

59

2. Exit that program.
3. Enter cc:Mail. Address the message normally.

4. With the cursor in the Message Contents section, press Alt-F9.   The `drive and directory` prompt line appears.

5. Backspace to remove the current line. Type in the drive, directory, and filename of the file you just saved.   The `starting from line` prompt appears.

6. Press Enter.   The `ending at line` prompt appears.

7. Press Enter.   The text of the file appears in the Message Contents area.   □

For example, assume you need to send a two-page memo to your work group outlining the current standard for attaching staples. You create the memo with your word processing software. As usual, you spell check the document (fixing several words) and then use a grammar checker. Once you are satisfied with the document, you save it as STAPLE01.DOC. This is the normal format.

Then you set the File Save option in your word processing program to `text only`, or something similar, and save it again as STAPLE01.TXT. This saves the file in the generic format. You can later return to the STAPLE01.DOC file if you need to make changes and reuse the file. The STAPLE01.TXT file is now ready to load into your cc:Mail text message.

Next, you start cc:Mail and use a mailing list you created to address the message to your work group. You enter the Subject: as New staple procedure. Now you are ready to load the text file STAPLE01.TXT. Press Alt-F9, and cc:Mail shows the current drive and directory. You can backspace to delete that information and then type the drive, directory, and filename. In this case, it might look like:

```
C:\WORD\DOCS\STAPLE01.TXT
```

When you press Enter, cc:Mail prompts you for the starting line number. Since you want to load the entire file, you just press Enter. You can also press Enter at the ending at line prompt. The entire STAPLE01.TXT document has now become a cc:Mail text message. To return to the Send menu, press F10.

60

> **Caution:** cc:Mail text items can only hold 20,000 characters, or approximately 24 screens of text. If your document exceeds that length, cc:Mail issues a message that the text buffer is full and cuts the document off.

Multi-Item Messages

The steps covered so far have created a single-item text message. However, cc:Mail messages can contain up to 20 different items, including DOS files and graphic images, which you attach from the Send menu. Chapter 2 covered these types of items. Chapter 6 explains how to attach them to a message.

Sending Messages

Once you have addressed the message and composed the text, you'll see the Send menu shown in Figure 3.7. From this menu you can add items, display and edit the message, and make changes to the address and subject lines. To send the message, you select `Send message`. Once you send the message, you return to the Main menu.

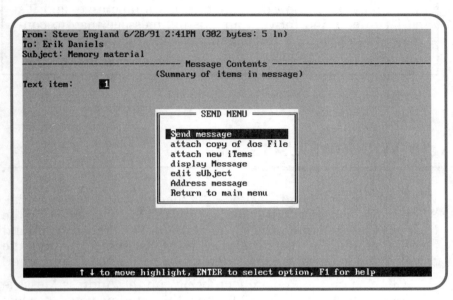

Figure 3.7   *The Send menu for attaching items and changing and sending the message.*

 Caution: If you return to the Main menu without sending the message, the contents will be lost.

The Message Log Feature

Normally when you send a message the only way to retain a copy is to copy the message to a folder, write it to an ASCII file, or archive it. But this involves an extra step that you have to remember to do.

If your system administrator has enabled the Message Log feature, however, this process is simple. You create a folder named "Message Log," and then all messages you send are also copied to that folder. You can then examine the contents of that folder just as you would with any other folder. To learn more about creating and using folders, see Chapter 4, "Dealing with Each Message."

> **Do you use a Message Log folder? Why or why not?**
>
> Yes. Many of the questions that arise are repetitive, and it's easier to edit and forward an existing message than to constantly be retyping. I archive all messages out of my Message Log folder every month.

For Windows Users

Windows users will find the process of sending mail less sequential. All the steps necessary are available from the Main window and the New Message window. Once you click on the Prepare icon and provide an address, the steps of entering the subject, setting the priority, and entering the messages can be performed in any order.

Clicking on the Prepare icon brings up the Address Message window, as shown in Figure 3.8. From this window you can select the way the Address box prefaces the name. The prefixes are TO: (the original recipient), CC: (courtesy copy), and BCC: (blind courtesy copy). The other recipients on the list don't see the names with the BCC designation.

You can also click on buttons to select from different lists. These include the main directory list, the public mailing lists created by your system administrator, your private mailing lists, the bulletin boards, and your folders.

After typing in the text in the Subject box, you must specifically select another element to complete. This is necessary because pressing Enter does not move you to another choice but just leaves the cursor in the Subject box. To move the cursor to the text editor, use the tab key.

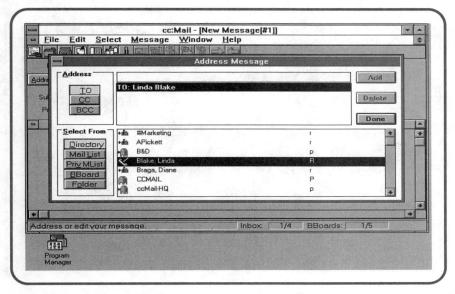

Figure 3.8   The Address Message window.

63

For any list, you double-click on a name to place it in the Address box. To see more names on the list, you can use the slider bar on the right edge of the list window. Or you can begin typing the name, and cc:Mail will point to the possible names. Once the name is filled in, you can click on the Add button or double-click on the name in the list.

You can select any name on any list to build the message address. If you make a mistake, select the name in the message list and click on the Delete button. Once the list is complete, click on the Done button and you'll return to the New Message window. If there are more names in the Address box than can be shown, a slider bar appears on the right side.

Once the address is complete, the New Message window appears as shown in Figure 3.9. The cursor starts in the Subject box. You can begin typing at that point to enter the subject text or move to one of the other parts of the message window.

The first step for creating messages can be changed under the Files Options Message choices. If you don't want to select the address first, you can designate the Subject, Text Editor, or even the Attach Dialog as the first actions. The Windows section in Chapter 5 provides more information on making these changes.

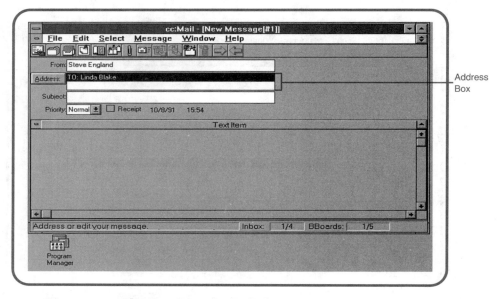

Address
Box

Figure 3.9   The New Message window.

To change the priority of the message, click on the Priority button in the New Message window. A list extends showing the Normal, Urgent, and Low priority selections. To change the current priority, click on a different priority in this list.

A return receipt can be toggled by clicking on the Receipt box. Click once to turn it on and an X appears in the box. Click again and the X is removed.

When you're ready to enter the text of the message, click on the Text Item window. The cursor begins blinking where the text will appear as you type. The editor is very similar to the Windows Write or Notepad editors. It allows insertions, deletions, and the use of the Edit pull-down menu. You can increase the size of the text editing window by clicking on the Maximize button in the upper right corner of that window.

You can also use the Windows Clipboard feature to bring text items into the editor. If you want to use graphic items from the Clipboard, you'll have to attach a graphic item to the message and paste from the Clipboard. The Attach, or Paper Clip, icon at the top of the screen also allows you to attach text, graphics, and files as additional items. This process is covered in Chapter 6, "Sending More Than Text."

To complete the process of sending a message, click on the Send icon. A confirmation window opens up. Click on Yes to send the message or No to return to the message being composed. Once the message is sent, the Prepare window closes and you are returned to the main cc:Mail screen.

What You Have Learned

► Messages can be addressed only to individuals on the post office mailing list.

► A message can be sent to more than one person at a time and to mailing lists, bulletin boards, and personal folders.

► The cc:Mail Editor program can create messages with up to 20,000 characters. It has some common word processing features and includes a special cc:Mail feature to highlight parts of the text message.

► Text files created with other word processing software can be easily loaded into a cc:Mail message.

► Messages can contain up to 20 items, including text, graphics, and DOS files.

► Messages can be set as Normal, Low, or Urgent priority.

► `Receipt Requested` will let you know when the recipient has read your message.

► If your system administrator has enabled the Message Log feature and you have created a Message Log folder, copies of all messages you send will also be copied to that folder.

65

Dealing with Each Message

In This Chapter

▶ *Replying to a message*
▶ *Forwarding a message*
▶ *Creating and using folders*
▶ *Saving files to disk*
▶ *Printing text and graphic items*

After you have read a message in your Inbox list, you will typically want to deal with it in some way. Many times you will respond to the message or forward it to someone else. Even if a response is not necessary, you may want to save the message to a folder. If you want to use the message as a DOS file, you can save the file in this format. You can print a message to your network or local printer. And, if the message has served its purpose and you need not keep a copy, you can delete it from your mailbox.

Replying to a Message

In many cases when you receive a message, you'll respond. cc:Mail makes the process of replying to messages easy by automatically addressing the message and retaining the contents of the subject line.

If you want to keep the original message and add your thoughts, you can edit the text immediately by pressing an Arrow key. If you want to compose a new message for the reply, pressing Enter returns you to the Action menu to select replY to message.

The first of two sets of Quick Steps below replies to a message by adding notes to the original. The second shows you how to start a new message as the reply.

 Replying by using the original message

1. After reading the message, press the Down Arrow key.

   The cursor appears in the Message Contents area.

2. Press the Ins key to insert the new text.

   The cursor changes to a blinking block instead of a line.

3. If you want your additional text to stand out from the original, press Alt-F1.

   This brings up the Highlight menu.

4. Use the Arrow keys to select a different color combination. Pressing the Down Arrow once will accomplish this.

   The highlight indicator at the bottom of the screen shows the next color combination.

5. Use the Arrow keys to reposition the cursor to where you want to add text. Type the additions.

   The text is inserted where you type.

6. Press F10 when finished.

   The Address menu appears on the screen. The highlight bar is on replY to sender.

7. Press Enter or Y.

   The Address menu appears again but the replY to sender choice is no longer available. The highlight is on eNd addressing.

8. Press Enter or N.	The Send menu appears. The highlight is on `Send message`.
9. Press Enter or S.	The message is sent. You return to your Inbox list to read the next message. □

Notice that these steps retain the original message. The next series of steps starts a new message.

Q Replying by creating a new message

1. After reading the message, press Enter.	The Action menu appears.
2. Select `reply to message`.	The message address reverses the names and keeps the same subject.
3. Type the message. Press F10 when you have completed the message.	The Send menu appears on the screen. The highlight bar is on `Send message`.
4. Press Enter or S.	The message is sent. You are returned to your Inbox list to read the next message. □

69

Remember that when using the original message as part of the reply, you need to move the cursor down into the Message Contents area and make some kind of change or addition. If you do not make a change, cc:Mail brings up the Action menu instead of the Address menu. Figure 4.1 shows a brief message sent about changes to a book and a possible lunch date. Note that the names of the sender and the recipient are not exchanged until after you press F10.

Once the recipient had read the message, he added comments to the message. Figure 4.2 illustrates how the Highlight feature emphasizes his new comments in the message. After finishing his response, he would press F10 to return to the Address menu, which would now highlight `reply to sender`.

At almost every step in the process of replying to a message, you can make changes or additions to the message or address, as described in Chapter 3. After adding to a message, you can attach more addresses, change the priority level, or request a receipt. Your original message may end up on a bulletin board or be sent to the entire post office mailing list!

Sender

Recipient

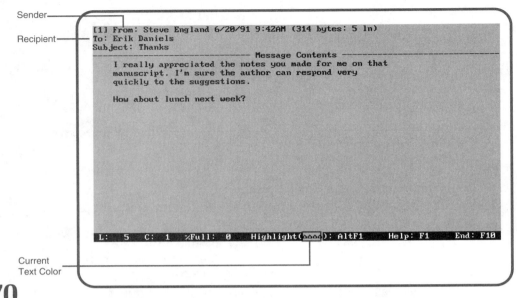

Current
Text Color

70

Figure 4.1   The original message.

New
Comments

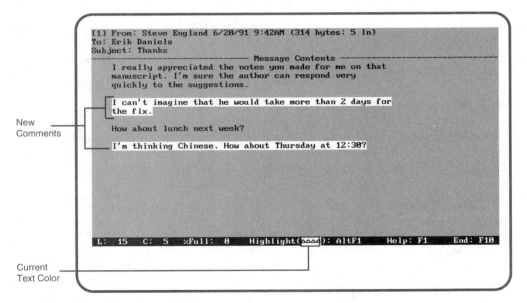

Current
Text Color

Figure 4.2   The original message with a response.

Tip: If you are not using a Message Log folder (see Chapter 3) to keep a copy of all your outgoing messages, add a folder address to your reply. This is a quick way to save the message in one of your folders with your new comments.

Of the messages you receive, how many require replies? How many exchanges are required to complete a topic?

Most messages I receive require a reply. The number of exchanges varies dramatically with the issue, but two or three is pretty common.

40 percent require a reply, and these may take several exchanges to complete.

Forwarding

Forwarding an e-mail message is similar to replying to a message. You can make changes to the text of a message and then send the message on to someone else. If you just want to forward the message, you can do this from the Action menu.

 Caution: If you make a change to the message before you use the Forward command, the address information from the previous sender is lost.

The following Quick Steps show you how to make changes to the message and keep the forwarding information intact.

Q **Forwarding a changed message**

1. After reading the message, press Enter.

The Action menu appears with display Next message highlighted.

2. Select Forward message.

The Address menu appears with Address to person highlighted.

3. Select eNd addressing. (You can add more addresses here if you want to forward to more than one person.)

The Send menu appears with Address message highlighted.

4. Select display Message.

The message appears on the screen with Forwarding lines added. The current To: line is empty.

5. Use the Down Arrow to move into the message area. Make additions as needed. Remember to use Alt-F1 to highlight text if desired. Press F10 to finish.

The Send menu appears with Address message highlighted.

6. Press Enter or A.

The Address menu appears with Address to person highlighted.

7. Use the Address menu to complete the top To: line of the message, adding names and mailing lists as necessary.

The Send menu appears with Send message highlighted.

8. Select eNd addressing.

9. Press Enter or S.

The message is sent, and you are returned to the Inbox list. □

If you just want to forward a message without making any comments or changes to the message, follow these Quick Steps.

 Forwarding a message

1. After reading the message, press Enter.

The Action menu appears with display Next message highlighted.

2. Select Forward message.

The Address menu appears with Address to person highlighted.

3. Select Address to person
   (or other type of address).

The Mailing Directory
appears.

4. Select the addresses. Press
   Esc when done.

The Address menu appears
with eNd addressing high-
lighted.

5. Press Enter or N.

The Send menu appears
with Send message high-
lighted.

6. Press Enter or S.

The message is sent, and
you are returned to the
Inbox list.   □

When you forward a message, you usually want the recipient to
see the path the message has taken. Figure 4.3 shows the expanded
address line with the original sender and recipient.

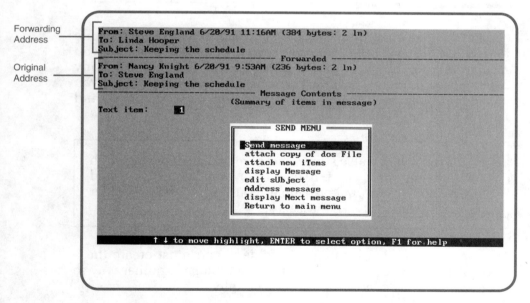

Figure 4.3   A forwarded message ready to send.

If you immediately make additions to the message by using an
Arrow key, the forwarding information will be lost and cc:Mail will
assume you're sending a new message. You can still send the
message to the new recipient, but the recipient won't know who
originated the message. Of course, you could always include a note
within the message explaining which part of the message is yours.

> **Do you usually forward a message with the original address or start the address line over?**
>
> Usually I use the Reply feature.
>
> Usually I forward with the original address, an old habit held over from mainframe-based mail. This allows tracking of the message's destinations.
>
> I start over.

Creating Folders

74

cc:Mail has an electronic filing system similar to the paper file folders in a filing cabinet. You can copy or move any message you receive in your Inbox to one or more folders. You can save any message you read on a bulletin board to a folder as well. Since you create and name the folders, you decide how many you need and what topics they will include.

> **Tip:** You can also store a message you are working on in a folder and recall it to change or send later. If you send similar messages to many people, you might create a folder containing these "stock" messages.

Before you store messages in folders, you must create these folders, as outlined in the following Quick Steps. Another way to create a folder is covered later in this chapter.

Creating one or more folders

1. From the Main menu, select Manage mailbox.

The Manage menu appears with manage Mailing lists highlighted at the top.

2. Select manage Folders.

The Folders screen appears, listing mailing lists on the left of the screen and bulletin boards/folders on the right. The highlight remains on the right side. The top of the screen shows the prompt Add new title or select existing folder:.

3. Type a new folder name and press Enter.

The new name is immediately added to the list.

4. Continue to type a new name for each folder.

Each name is added to the list in alphabetical order.

5. If you make a mistake, type the folder name or move the highlight to that folder name and press Enter.

A Folder menu appears to change, delete, or select another title. The highlight is on Change folder title.

6. Press Enter or C.

The folder title appears at the top of the screen.

7. Make changes as necessary and press Enter.

The new folder title is replaced in the list.

8. To end the process, press Esc.

The Manage menu appears.

9. Press Esc again or select Return to main menu.

The Main menu appears on the screen. □

> **Caution:** You will receive just one caution prompt from cc:Mail if you choose to delete a folder from the Folder menu. When a folder is deleted, all the messages in that folder are also deleted.

The Folders screen also contains the post office mailing lists, the bulletin boards, and your private mailing lists. When working from the manage Folders menu selection, you can use the highlight only on the right side of the screen, as shown in Figure 4.4. The titles at the top of the list, beginning with #, are the post office's bulletin boards. Only the system administrator can change those titles.

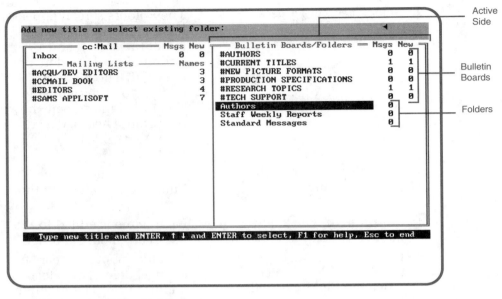

Figure 4.4 The Folders screen.

Your folder names can be uppercase or lowercase and can be up to 30 characters long. They are arranged in alphabetical order. You can have up to 200 folders with up to 1,600 messages in each one. This provides you with space for 320,000 messages.

Just like your file drawers, your folders can be organized on the basis of how much material you need to manage in a day or week. The more folders you create, the more structured your system for naming and using them should be. Here are some tips for folder management:

▶ Since you need to type the folder name only once, use as many of the 30 characters as possible to create descriptive folder names.

▶ Remember that the list is automatically alphabetized. You can add new folder names at any time, and they'll be placed where you can find them quickly.

▶ Think of the list as an outline in which each level must be repeated on each folder. For example, instead of assigning separate folders on your list to three staff members named Knight, Right, and White, call these folders STAFF—Knight, STAFF—Right, and STAFF—White. The folders will then be grouped together on the list.

▶ Once a project is over, you can archive the messages to disk and delete the folder. You can always access the archived messages on disk.

▶ Use the search-by-date function on all your folders at one time to archive messages. This can be done every six months or more often, depending on the number of messages you manage.

▶ If a message contains a DOS file that you copy to your disk, you may not need to keep that item as part of the message. You'll save post office space by deleting that item from the message before moving the message to your folder.

▶ If you have trouble remembering what goes in a file, create a message for each folder called CONTENTS. Make a note to yourself explaining what kinds of messages go in the folder. If you forget, select reTrieve messages and then search by Keyword phrase from the Folder menu to scan the message headings for each folder message called CONTENTS.

77

 How many folders do you have? What are some of them called? How many messages do you handle in a week?

I have about 20 folders. I separate messages that I want to refer back to by topic (in my case, by product line).

Usually about 6 to 10 folders. The titles vary from week to week depending upon what I'm working on at the time. I may receive anywhere from 20 to 100 messages per week.

No folders. We generally handle 30 to 50 messages weekly.

Another Way to Create Folders

You can also create folders instantly when you want to copy or move a message to a folder that does not yet exist. You just type the full name of the new folder and press Enter. No warning message pops up on the screen as it does when you type a nonexistent name in a mailing list. The folder is automatically created and the message copied or moved to that new folder name.

If you should mistype a folder name, for example,   `Staff nots` instead of `Staff notes` , you will slightly misplace the message in your alphabetized folder list. If, on the other hand, you mistakenly type `Dtaff notes` , the folder will be located much higher in the list, and the message might be lost until you discover the accidentally created folder.

Saving Messages in Folders

Messages from the Inbox can be saved by moving or copying them to one or more folders. Those messages that are moved are taken off the Inbox list, whereas those that are copied remain on the list. In either case, however, the basic steps for moving or copying messages to one or more folders are the same.

 Moving a message to a folder

1. After reading a message, press Enter.

   The Action menu appears with `display Next message` highlighted.

2. Select `Move to folder`.

   Your list of folders is highlighted in the upper right corner of the screen.

3. Begin typing the first few letters of the folder name or move the pointer to the folder name.

   As you type the letters, the highlight moves to the folder name beginning with those letters.

4. When the folder you want to keep the message in is highlighted, press Enter.

   The message is moved to that folder. When you return to the Inbox list, that message line is gone.   □

After you select `Move to folder` or `Copy to folder` in step 2, you'll see the screen shown in Figure 4.5. The right part of the screen contains your list of folders. Once you select the folder by highlighting it and pressing Enter, the screen returns to the Action menu. From here you can copy or move the message to another folder. If the message is still in the Inbox, you can use `Delete message` on the Action menu to remove it.

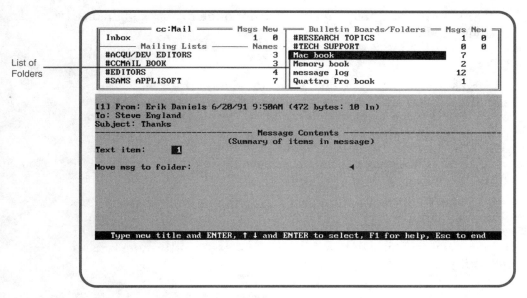

List of
Folders

Figure 4.5   The list of folders on the Folders screen.

79

After the message is in a folder, it can still be recalled and used like any message. However, by moving an Inbox message to a folder you cannot reply to the message as easily. You have to address that message back to the sender. To avoid this potential problem, reply to the message first and then move it to the folder.

The only difference between moving and copying messages to a folder is that a copy of the message remains in the first location when you choose the copy sequence. If you want to store the message in several folders, you need to repeat the Copy to folder sequence for each folder.

Saving to Disk

The cc:Mail post office resides on a network computer, most likely the network host. All the data files are kept in a specific directory and are used by everyone who has a mailbox defined in the post office. Although no one has access to your messages or folders except the system administrator, the files are still vulnerable to many kinds of network disasters. Those data files are undoubtedly backed up on a regular schedule and could be recovered if need be. But having copies of critical files on your hard disk or on floppy disks is still a good idea.

cc:Mail provides several ways to save entire messages and specific message items to disk. One way is to save a text message item as an ASCII file, a generic file format that can be used by all word processing software. (See Chapter 3 for a more complete discussion of ASCII files.) If you want to reuse the contents of a text message in your word processing package, you start by saving the message in ASCII format.

To keep copies of your messages in a more compact and secure form, cc:Mail can archive messages to a file on the disk. You may want to think of the archive file as a folder—except that you keep that folder in a warehouse, where it's safer but takes a little more time to get to if you need it.

80

Writing to an ASCII File

Messages are written to an ASCII file from the Action menu. You can perform this action to a message currently in the Inbox, a message you just read, or a message from a folder or bulletin board. Any text message item can be sent to an ASCII file.

In most cases you would save the file to your local disk or to another area of the system. Once a message has been saved as an ASCII file, anyone can read that file. The following Quick Steps show you how to save a text message as an ASCII file.

Q **Saving a file to ASCII format**

1. After reading the message, select Write to ascii file.

   The current drive and subdirectory containing the Mail program are displayed.

2. Backspace to clear the prompt. Then type in the drive, directory, and filename you want and press Enter.

   A notation appears that the message is being saved. The Action menu returns.

   □

After you exit cc:Mail, you can then load your word processing software. To load the file, you type the same drive, directory, and filename you used to save the file. Figure 4.6 shows the text message. Figure 4.7 shows the message as an ASCII file.

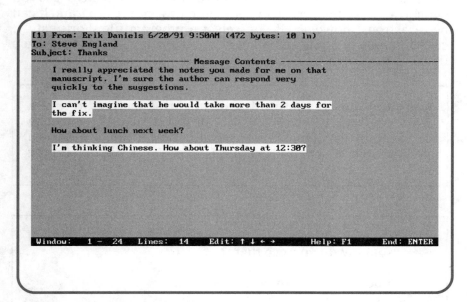

Figure 4.6   The text message to be saved as ASCII file.

```
E:\>type note.txt

[1] From: Erik Daniels 6/20/91 9:50AM (472 bytes: 10 ln)
To: Steve England
Subject: Thanks
------------------------- Message Contents -----------------------------

    I really appreciated the notes you made for me on that
    manuscript. I'm sure the author can respond very
    quickly to the suggestions.

    I can't imagine that he would take more than 2 days for
    the fix.

    How about lunch next week?

    I'm thinking Chinese. How about Thursday at 12:30?
♀
E:\>
```

Figure 4.7   The text message after being saved as an ASCII file.

cc:Mail also allows you to write an ASCII file to the end of an existing file. You simply highlight the filename you want to use and press Enter. This works well if you have three different messages you want to add together to use in your word processing program. It can be disastrous, however, if you select a program file. Fortunately, cc:Mail protects itself and will not let you create a file with the same name as its program filenames.

 Caution: If you use the highlighting method to save a message to an ASCII file on the hard disk, you may accidentally save the file under a different name or destroy a program file. The safest method is to save the file to a floppy disk.

Do you save many messages to disk in ASCII format? If so, how do you use them?

Yes, I put them in an indexed textbase.

Yes, but only when the body of the message contains information that we may want to import into other programs.

Archiving Messages

Like a file drawer you never clean out, your electronic message folders can accumulate a lot of old messages. Routinely deleting unneeded messages saves disk space and keeps the number of messages manageable. But if you delete all those saved messages with the Delete message command, you'll never be able to refer back to them.

Instead of throwing that information away, you can archive those messages. The Action menu provides an archiVe message choice. When messages are archived, they are saved to a separate disk file, typically somewhere else in the system or on your own disk.

These archived messages are then readily available from the reTrieve messages choice in the Main menu. They can be read and handled just like any other messages. The following Quick Steps show you how to archive all your messages that fall before a specific date and then delete those messages from your mailbox.

Q Archiving messages by date

1. From the Main menu, select reTrieve messages.

   The Retrieve menu appears with retrieve from bboard/Folder highlighted.

2. Select search by Calendar date.

   The screen shows the total number of messages selected so far and prompts for the on or after date.

3. Press Enter to leave this date blank.

   That prompt is replaced by the on or before date prompt.

4. Type a date for the oldest message you want to leave in all your folders using the mm/dd/yy format.

   The system selects those messages that were sent on or before the date you specified. The number of messages selected is updated and the Retrieve menu appears.

5. Select Act on messages.

   The Action menu appears with Move to folder highlighted.

6. Select archiVe messages.

   The current DOS drive and directory appears.

7. Backspace to clear the line and type the drive, directory, and filename for the archive file.

   The Action menu appears. The messages are still selected.

8. Select Delete messages.

   The program prompts: Are you sure ...?

9. Press Y and then Enter.

   The same messages just copied to the archive file have been deleted from your mailbox. The Action menu appears again.

10. Select Return to main menu.

    The Main menu appears. □

83

As in any effort to manage data, you need to be consistent when archiving files. Note that the archive filename is limited to eight characters, plus three for the extension. You might want to use the three-character extension to identify the file as a cc:Mail archive file.

For example, you could use the extensions CCM or ACV, as in PROJ.CCM or PROJ.ACV, where PROJ might indicate the name of the project that the archived files relate to.

cc:Mail can also add messages to an existing archive file. Once you start a file, you can just keep adding messages to it. As a file grows larger, however, it will take you more time to find messages.

> **Caution:** If you save your archive on the host computer, anyone with access to that drive or directory who uses cc:Mail can read that file. The most secure location for an archive file is your local hard disk or, even better, a floppy disk that you can keep locked up.

Although the previous Quick Steps searched for files by date, you can use any combination of search methods to archive your files. For example, if you have your messages organized in folders, you can archive each folder by name and date. On the first of each month, you might select each folder in turn and then select messages older than three months to archive. Your individual archive files would then add the messages from four months ago.

You might also keep your messages in folders by project. When you archive those messages, you can select individual names for the search method. The archive file can then use these names as filenames. For example, Nancy Knight might be saved as KNIGHTN.CCM.

In general, the easiest way to maintain your archive files is to follow the basic procedure outlined in the previous Quick Steps. Once a month select all messages older than three months and save them to an archive file. Make sure you delete those same files from your mailbox. And always make sure you use the same time interval, three months or six months or whatever you choose, whenever you perform the archive process.

To use archived messages, the archive file must be available from the network host or local drive. If the archive file is on a floppy disk, make sure the disk is inserted in the drive. The following Quick Steps show you how to locate and use an old message from an archived file.

Do you have and use a system to archive your messages?

Yes, we archive monthly.

No. All messages are either rerouted or purged as soon as possible.

Q Finding and using an archived message

1. From the Main menu select reTrieve messages.	The Retrieve menu appears.
2. Select retrieve from archiVe file.	The current drive and file directory appear.
3. Type the drive, directory, and filename for the archive file.	Depending on the size of the file, cc:Mail may take a moment to read the file. The Retrieve menu appears.
4. Select one of the five search methods and enter the appropriate search key.	The Retrieve menu reappears for further actions. ☐

85

Once you have read the archive file, you can use it just like a folder or bulletin board, with one exception—you cannot delete messages from it. You can copy messages from the archive file back into folders again if you want to return those messages to the mailbox.

 Tip: If you want to remove messages from an archive file, search the file for the messages you want to keep. Then save those messages to a new archive file and delete the old archive file.

Printing Messages

With the exception of DOS files, all message items can be printed to a printer. The resulting quality will depend on the type of printer used. The system administrator has established a default (normal) printer for everyone using cc:Mail. Where your printed output ends up will depend on this setting and the physical location of the printer.

You can change those settings from the Profile menu. For example, the cc:Mail default may be to print to the LPT1: port with an HP Laserjet attached to that port. Since this port is a network printer, you may have to walk down the hall to pick up your printed output. If you have your own printer on the LPT2: port, however, you can change that system default, as outlined in the following Quick Steps.

Q Setting the printer

1. From the Main menu, select `Manage mailbox`.	The Manage menu appears.
2. Select `Change profile`.	The Profile menu appears.
3. Select `change Printer port`.	An Options list appears.
4. Select your local printer port.	You are returned to the Profile menu.
5. Select `change printer Type`.	An Options list appears.
6. Select the choice for your printer. If you are not sure, choose `Text only`.	The Profile menu appears. Note your current printer settings in the upper right corner.
7. Select `Return to main menu`.	The Main menu appears. ☐

If, after making these changes, your printer does not work as expected, you may want to try different printer ports. If you have a graphics printer and want to print graphics, you have to select the IBM or one of the two HP choices on the menu. (The *Fine Resolution* option provides higher quality output but also increases printing time.). To return to the original settings created by the system administrator, select the `Default` choices under each of the Options lists.

Figure 4.8 shows the Profile menu. This menu also allows you to change your password, your highlight default, and your margin default. More information on these settings is available in Chapter 5, "Managing Your Mailbox."

To print a message item, select `Print message` from the Action menu. If the printer is not turned on or is off-line, a cc:Mail error message appears stating that the `Printer is unavailable`. The message can be cleared by pressing the Esc key. Correct the printer problem and try again.

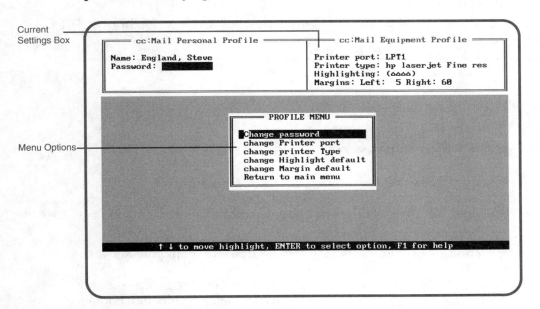

Current Settings Box

Menu Options

Figure 4.8   The Profile menu.

87

Tip: If you do not have access to a printer but want printed copies of your message, use the `Write to ascii file` selection on the Action menu. You can use word processing software later to load and print the message.

Do you routinely print copies of messages for your files? Why or why not?

Never. That's what computers are for. If I print a message I have to file it and then look through the file. It's much more convenient to use a keyword search to locate what I'm looking for.

Generally I print only the messages that have information I need to have at hand when I'm away from the office or a PC.

Yes. For technical support calls, messages are filed for future reference.

88 Deleting Messages

Messages can be deleted immediately after they are read or after they have been placed in folders. Once deleted, a message can be recovered only if it has been archived or backed up on tape (see Chapter 5).

You can also delete messages in groups after using the Retrieve menu to search for those messages. Simply follow the pattern outlined in the Quick Steps earlier in this chapter in the section "Archiving Messages." The files to be removed are selected, copied to an archive file, and then deleted.

 What percentage of messages do you delete immediately as opposed to saving to a folder?

90 percent of the messages I receive get deleted after I've read or responded to them. I save what I've sent (in my Message Log) and archive or file that.

75 percent.

Virtually all, say, 90 percent.

For Windows Users

The Windows icons across the top of the cc:Mail screen make it easy to reply to and forward messages. Any time you are reading a message, the Reply and Forward icons change from grey (nonfunctional) to colored.

To reply to a message, click on the Reply icon or press ALT-Y. The message box appears, as shown in Figure 4.9. If you click on Retain the Original Item to remove the X, the original message is cleared off. If you leave the X, the original message remains. Once you select Yes, the From: and Address: lines are exchanged. You can make changes to the message, if you kept it, and then click on the Send icon.

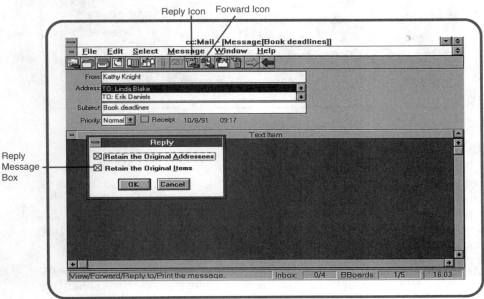

Figure 4.9   The Reply window prompt.

The Forward icon takes the message you are reading and allows you to send it to someone else. After clicking on the Forward icon or pressing Alt-R, the Forward Message box appears, as shown in Figure 4.10. If you reply Yes, the From: line is replaced with your name and the Address Message dialog box opens up. You then select one or more addresses to forward the message to. Messages forwarded as New do not retain the original header information. Therefore, if you select No, the recipient will have to click on the From button to see who sent and received the original.

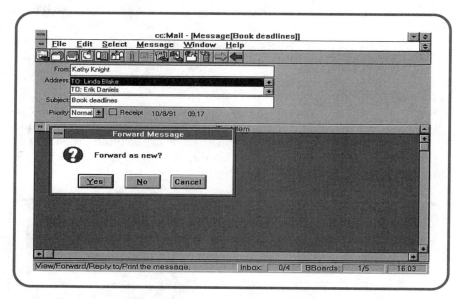

Figure 4.10   The Forward Message box.

To print a message, click on the File choice on the menu bar by or press Alt-F. From that pull-down menu, select Print. The message item will be sent to the default printer. If you need to change the printer, select Printer Setup on that same File menu. Notice that the printed message does not include the address names and dates but only the text of the message.

Any selected message can be copied or moved to Folders or Archive files by selecting the Store message icon or by selecting Store Message from the File menu. Alt-T also brings up the Store Message dialog box shown in Figure 4.11. The messages can be moved or copied to a folder or to a new or existing Archive file.

For example, once a message has been read, you can select the Store message icon to bring up the dialog box. Click on the folder you want to move the message to and click on OK. Because you are moving the message, you are prompted to confirm the deletion of the message from the Inbox list. The message is now in the designated folder.

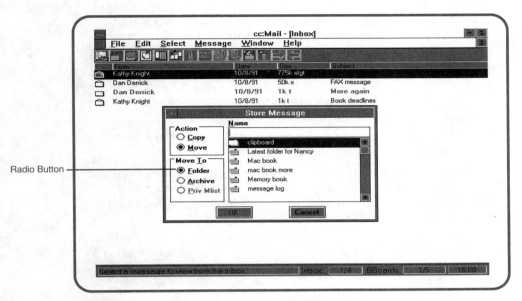

Radio Button

Figure 4.11   The Store Message Dialog Box.

91

To save space and keep a permanent record of your messages, you may also want to Store messages from Folders to Archive files. Make sure you read the DOS section for covering archive files. With cc:Mail for Windows, you just select the messages with the Shift or Control keys and then open the Store Messages dialog box. All the marked messages are then saved to the archive file you designate.

What You Have Learned

► When you reply to a message, cc:Mail exchanges the To: and From: names. You can make changes to the same message, or you can create a new message.

► If you want make changes when forwarding a message and still retain the original address information, you have to forward the message and then return to the text items to make the changes.

▶ You can save all the messages you send and receive in folders. You create and name the folders based on your message storage needs.

▶ Individual messages and groups of messages can be saved to archive files on another disk, usually your own. These files can also be searched and retrieved just like messages in the Inbox and in your folders.

▶ Text message items can be saved as ASCII (text) files to be used with your word processing software.

▶ You can print all text items to the default printer. If you want to print to a local printer, you may have to make changes to the printer setup. If you have a graphics printer, you can also print graphic items.

▶ Once you delete a message, it is gone from the post office. A good strategy is to archive important messages to your disk first before deleting them.

92

Chapter 5

Managing Your Mailbox

In This Chapter

93

► *Creating and changing mailing lists*
► *Using (and abusing) mailing lists*
► *Maintaining message security*
► *Changing your password*
► *Resetting highlights and margins*

As a cc:Mail user in a post office, you have a mailbox. Messages are left in your mailbox when other users send mail to your address, usually your name. This electronic version of a mailbox is very different from the paper version. Much more than a small box with a door at one end, your mailbox contains folders to keep your mail as well as your own personal mailing lists. Chapter 4 showed you how to create and save messages in your folders. In this chapter, you'll cover the other ways you can manage your mailbox.

Managing Mailing Lists

Your system administrator may have created one or more public mailing lists. These lists contain a number of addresses from your local or remote post offices. Anyone can address a message to all the people in this list just by placing the mailing list name in the address portion of the message. You can also create personal mailing lists for your own "mass mailings."

Creating a List

You create a mailing list in the same way you address a message. You simply select names from the public mailing list, and they are added to your personal mailing list, as shown in the following Quick Steps.

94

 Creating a mailing list

1. From the Main menu, select Manage mailbox.	The Manage menu appears with the highlight on manage Mailing lists.
2. Press Enter or M.	The Mailing Lists screen appears listing mailing lists on the left and bulletin boards/folders on the right. The highlight remains on the Mailing Lists side.
3. Type a name, up to 30 characters, for the mailing list and press Enter.	The mailing directory appears.
4. Move to the name you want to include in your personal mailing list and press Enter.	That name appears at the top of the screen.
5. Continue to select names to add to the mailing list. Press Esc when done.	The Mailing Lists screen reappears.
6. Press Esc.	The Manage menu reappears.
7. Select Return to main menu.	The Main menu appears. □

The screen displayed in Figure 5.1 serves a dual purpose. In this case, only the left side is active, showing the list of mailing lists. The public mailing lists begin with #. Your mailing lists will appear below those public lists. The other side contains the bulletin boards and your folders and is accessed from the Folder menu, as described in the "Creating Folders" section of Chapter 4.

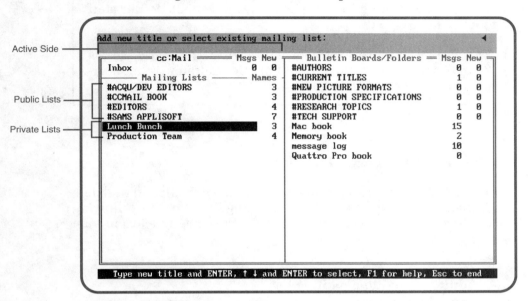

Figure 5.1   The Mailing Lists screen.

95

As you build your list by selecting names from the mailing directory, you can either highlight and Enter each name or you can begin typing the first few letters of the name. As your letters match a name, the highlight narrows the choices in the alphabetized list. If you continue to type a name that is not on the list, the program provides a warning message.

> ⚡ **Do you have many private mailing lists? What kinds of messages do you send?**
>
> We have about one dozen lists, typically for short term projects.
>
> We send everything from system announcements to our staff hockey team schedule.
>
> Yes, we have close to 30 private mailing lists. Generally, we use them to send company-confidential information to other business partners across the country.

Changing Addresses in the List

96

Once you have created a private mailing list, you can add or delete addresses and change or delete the mailing list title. The following two sets of Quick Steps show you how to make changes to a private mailing list.

 Adding names to a mailing list

1. From the Main menu, select `Manage mailbox`.	The Manage menu appears with the highlight on `manage Mailing lists`.
2. Press Enter or M.	The Mailing Lists screen appears listing mailing lists on the left and bulletin boards/folders on the right. The highlight remains on the Mailing Lists side.
3. Begin typing a name for your mailing list or move the highlight to that name. Press Enter.	The Mailing List menu appears with `View mailing list` highlighted.
4. Select `Add names to mailing list`.	The public mailing directory appears with the list of current names in your private list.

5. Select the name to add and press Enter.

The name is added to the list at the top of the screen.

6. Continue to select names to add to the mailing list. Press Esc when done.

The Mailing List menu reappears.

7. Select `Return to mail menu`.

The Main menu appears. □

 Erasing names from a mailing list

1. From the Main menu, select `Manage mailbox`.

The Manage menu appears with the highlight on `manage Mailing lists`.

2. Press Enter or M.

The Mailing Lists screen appears listing mailing lists on the left and bulletin boards/folders on the right. The highlight remains on the Mailing Lists side.

97

3. Begin typing the name of your mailing list you want to change or move the highlight to that name. Press Enter.

The Mailing List menu appears with `View mailing list` highlighted.

4. Select `Erase names from mailing list`.

The current names in the mailing list appear.

5. Use the Arrow keys to point to the name to erase and press Enter. Press Esc when finished erasing names.

The Mailing List menu reappears.

□

When making changes to a mailing list, you can only add or erase names. You cannot retype someone's name. If a name is changed or deleted on the post office mailing directory, that name will also be changed or deleted in your private mailing list.

The Mailing List menu, shown in Figure 5.2, also allows you to change the title or delete the mailing list entirely. When changing a title, you see the old title at the top of the screen. To make your changes you use the Right and Left Arrows and the Backspace key.

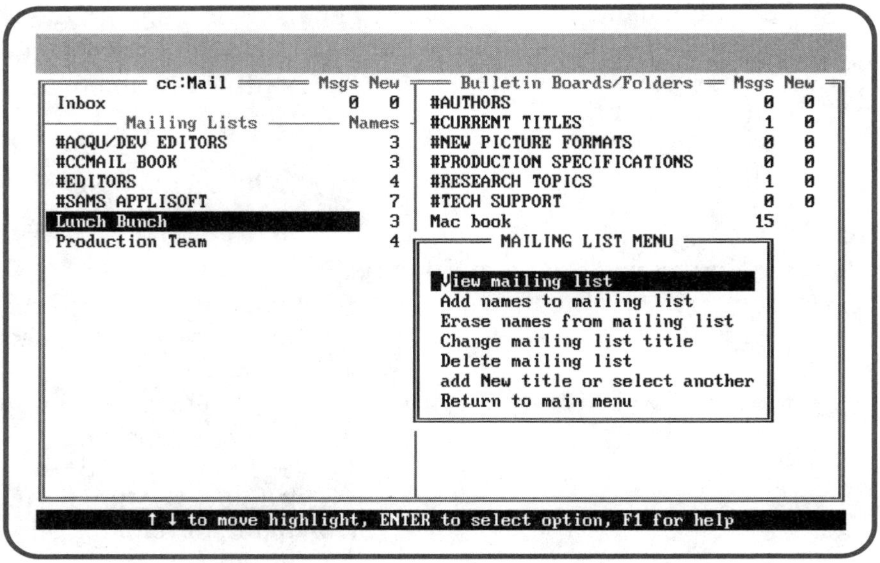

```
┌─────── cc:Mail ═══════ Msgs New ┌── Bulletin Boards/Folders ══ Msgs New ┐
│ Inbox                    0   0  │ #AUTHORS                        0   0 │
│ ──── Mailing Lists ──── Names ─ │ #CURRENT TITLES                 1   0 │
│ #ACQU/DEV EDITORS            3  │ #NEW PICTURE FORMATS            0   0 │
│ #CCMAIL BOOK                 3  │ #PRODUCTION SPECIFICATIONS      0   0 │
│ #EDITORS                     4  │ #RESEARCH TOPICS                1   0 │
│ #SAMS APPLISOFT              7  │ #TECH SUPPORT                   0   0 │
│ Lunch Bunch                  3  │ Mac book                       15      │
│ Production Team              4  │ ┌════ MAILING LIST MENU ════════┐ │
│                                 │ │ View mailing list              │ │
│                                 │ │ Add names to mailing list      │ │
│                                 │ │ Erase names from mailing list  │ │
│                                 │ │ Change mailing list title      │ │
│                                 │ │ Delete mailing list            │ │
│                                 │ │ add New title or select another│ │
│                                 │ │ Return to main menu            │ │
│                                 │ │                                │ │
│                                 │ └────────────────────────────────┘ │
│        ↑↓ to move highlight, ENTER to select option, F1 for help       │
```

Figure 5.2   The Mailing List menu.

Before allowing you to delete a mailing list, the program displays the prompt Are you sure you wish to delete the mailing list? As soon as you press Y, that list is removed from the Mailing List screen. Pressing N returns you to the Mailing List menu. Once deleted, a mailing list cannot be recovered. There is no way to archive or share your private mailing lists.

Using (and Abusing) Mailing Lists

Sending an e-mail message to hundreds of mailboxes is as easy as sending a message to one. For this reason, users may be inclined to abuse mailing lists. The larger the post office, the more likely "junk" messages will be sent to your mailbox. The more users, the higher the chance of getting e-junk from people who use public and private mailing lists too liberally.

To keep from creating your own e-junk, consider the type of message you're sending and the audience you're addressing. If the message contains information necessary for everyone to know or act upon, you may need to use the department level mailing list. If, on the other hand, you are making a minor request, it is more appropriate to post the message on a bulletin board.

Although you know who is in the mailing lists you create, the content of the public mailing lists may not be obvious. For example, does `#Accounting Dept.` mean the managers or everyone in the department? When you select a public mailing list under the Manage menu, you can view the names on that list. Then you can identify at least a few of the names in the group you send messages to.

If you receive e-junk messages, you can provide a gentle reminder to the sender that you don't want to get that kind of mail. Rather than immediately deleting the message, use `Reply` and attach a note to the bottom of the message. It need not be harsh—just a polite suggestion that the user consider sending this kind of message to a bulletin board instead. Even if only a few people respond, the sender should begin to understand that these kinds of messages are not well received.

Naturally you take a risk when responding that way. E-mail has been available for only a few years, and not everyone is yet familiar with e-mail etiquette. By providing a gentle reminder, you help everyone learn. And, in turn, if you receive a such a message, don't take the response personally. Instead, consider this type of response the e-mail equivalent of a yawning audience. Of course, you will read every message the president of the company sends out, won't you?

99

Message Security

The post office directory contains the message database and other files. All these files are stored in a special format that only the cc:Mail program can use. The only way to access your mailbox is to use your password. Remember, if anyone learns your password, they can read your mail and send messages under your name. Therefore, as discussed in Chapter 1, always create a password that only you know.

> **Tip:** If you should ever forget your password, don't panic. The system administrator can always reset your password so that you can log in. You can then change your password to something you can remember.

Your message files are also vulnerable when you save files as ASCII and archive files. Remember that ASCII files can be used with any word processing software. If you save a message item as an ASCII file and store it on the network, anyone with access to that same area can read that file without your knowledge. Likewise, anyone with access to cc:Mail can enter your archive file if it's kept on the network. cc:Mail does not determine if the address (your name) using the archive file is the same as the address that created it.

Therefore, when using ASCII and archive files, your best method of security is to keep the files on a local hard drive or floppy disk. Saving your files on a hard disk limits their access to others using that computer. Floppy disk storage is even more effective, since you can easily remove the disk and lock it in a safe place.

When you delete a message in cc:Mail, it cannot be recovered. It is up to you, the user, to save important messages to an archive or ASCII file before you delete them. Depending on the backup schedule and the method used on the network host, those files might remain available for weeks or months.

For example, all the data files might be saved weekly to tape. Those backup tapes are rotated every six months. If you delete a message on Monday from the previous Thursday, the message will still be contained on the backup tape created Friday night. That tape will be available for six months until it is reused for another backup.

In all matters of message security and message privacy, you should consult your system administrator. Recent litigation suggests that company mail is not private and may be used against employees in a court of law. You should request a written policy statement to make clear what may and may not be included in company e-mail messages.

> **What kinds of security precautions do you take? Does your company have a written policy about message contents?**
>
> The encrypt inherent in cc:Mail, combined with the password, is sufficient for my needs.
>
> Security is based on the user's network password and the user's cc:Mail password. Administrators are very few and are aware of the sensitivity of all types of mail: personal, electronic, or otherwise. Mail database export facilities are secured and are generally not used at present.
>
> I'm unable to answer. I don't know!

101

Changing Your Profile

Besides your personal mailing lists and folders, your mailbox has a unique profile that includes your password, your highlight and margin defaults, and your printer port and printer type. You can change most of your profile from the Profile menu (see Figure 4.8), which you access through the Manage menu. To set your printer port and printer type, see Chapter 4, "Dealing with Each Message."

Your password is one part of your profile that you may want to change occasionally as a security precaution. You do this by selecting Change password from the Profile menu. In order to choose a new password, you must first type in your old password. This prevents someone from sitting down in front of your system when you step out and making changes you would not want. (See the section "Your Password" in Chapter 1 for more information on choosing a password.)

If you wish to change your highlight default, you have three choices available from the Default Highlight menu. Last highlight set is the default, which retains the last color combination set. Suppose, for example, that you reply to a message and change the highlight to white letters on a black background. You type your comments on the message and send it. The next message you create will use that same highlight setting, white on black.

A second choice, User default, brings up the color examples shown in Figure 5.3. The lower right corner of the screen shows the current setting for all text. The Up and Down Arrows change the background color, and the Right and Left Arrows change the text color. When you establish a preferred color combination, press Enter. The upper right corner of the screen now shows the current text color that will be used in your messages.

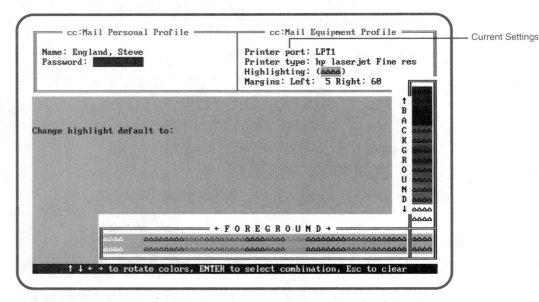

Figure 5.3   The Color Combination Select menu.

Finally, Post office default sets the text colors to the combination used as the system default, which is set by the system administrator. You can see the current colors in the upper right corner of the screen.

> **Tip:** Just because there are 128 possible combinations does not mean they are all good to use. Many of them are not very comfortable to read. The most common are white or bright white on blue. Yellow on blue is also easy to read.

To change your margin default, you follow the same pattern as when changing the highlight default. After selecting change Margin default on the Profile menu, you'll have two settings to choose from. The standard setting, Last margins set, retains the changes from the last message and applies them to new messages. To create a new user default, select User default. The screen shown in Figure 5.4 displays the left and right margin markers for you to change.

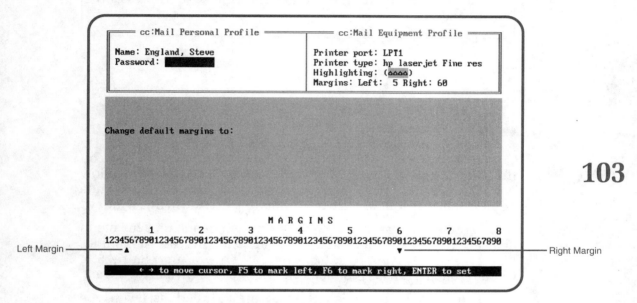

103

Figure 5.4   The Change Margin Default screen.

As noted at the bottom of the screen, F5 sets the left margin and F6 sets the right margin. To change these settings, use the Right and Left Arrows to position the cursor. Then press F5 or F6, depending on the margin you want to set. Press Enter to return to the Profile menu.

> **Tip:** A very wide screen of text may be hard to read. A setting of 5 and 60 will be easier to read and appear more friendly as well.

What have you changed your text color or margin settings to?

I change them frequently to contrast with whatever I'm replying to. (His survey response was in orange.)

My screen has a blue background with white text. Margins are at 10 and 70.

For Windows Users

To create a private mailing list in cc:Mail for Windows, you click on the Priv Mlist icon or press Alt-V. The Private Mailing Lists window opens and displays all the private lists you have created. To examine any list, you can double-click on the mailing list title in this window.

To create a new mailing list, select the File menu. This menu changes to reflect the current open window. In this case, it includes `Create/Rename Private Mailing List`, as shown in Figure 5.5. Clicking on that choice produces the dialog box shown in Figure 5.6.

The Create/Rename dialog box serves two functions. If you type in the current name of a mailing list, you can rename this list by typing a new name on the `To:` line. If you type in a new name for a mailing list, that name is added to the Private Mailing Lists window after you click on the Create button.

To add names to a new mailing list, open both the Private Mailing List window and the Directory window. You may have to rearrange and resize the windows to get a good view of both of them. Figure 5.7 shows an arrangement to provide the most information from the directory and still show the names in the list. To copy names, click on the name in the Directory window and drag the name to the Mailing List window.

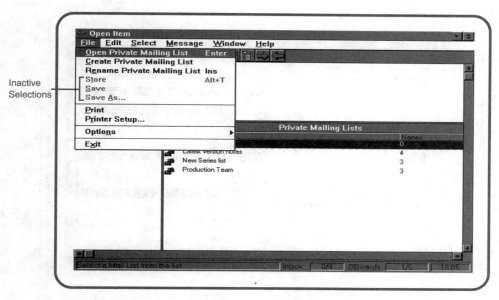

Inactive
Selections

Figure 5.5   The File menu for the Private Mailing List window.

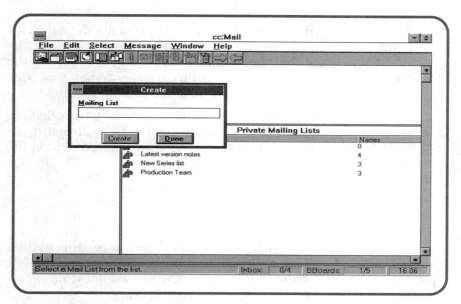

Figure 5.6   The Dialog Box to Create a Private Mailing List.

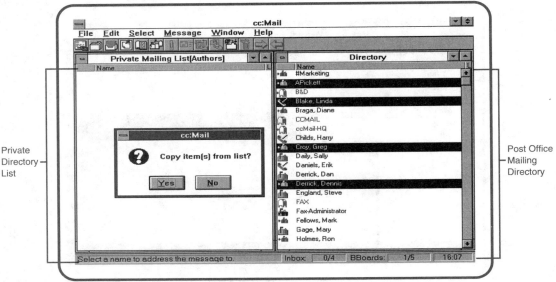

Figure 5.7 A possible arrangement of windows before copying addresses from the directory to a private mailing list.

Private Directory List

Post Office Mailing Directory

To select more than one name at a time, press down on the Ctrl key while selecting the names. When you have selected all the names to copy, click and drag from the Directory window to the Mailing List window. A confirmation box appears. When you click on Yes, the names will be copied over to the private mailing list.

You can delete a name from this private mailing list by selecting the name and pressing Del or using Delete in the Edit menu. To delete multiple names and mailing lists, simply hold down on the Ctrl key while making your selections.

Setting Options

Windows users have a wide variety of choices relating to their profile. This includes changing the password, changing the display, setting confirmations, and selecting display fonts. Figure 5.8 shows the Options menu available from the File menu.

The Change Password dialog box on this menu asks for the old password and the new password. After typing in the old password for confirmation, use the Tab key or click on the new password box. Enter the new password and press Enter. The next time you start cc:Mail, you'll use that password.

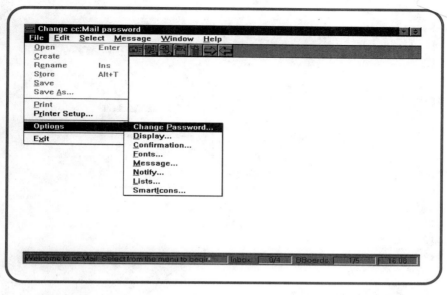

Figure 5.8   The Options menu available from the File menu.

The Display Options window, shown in Figure 5.9, shows the many changes you can make to the cc:Mail program. When first installed, all the check boxes are marked. These represent all the possible options. Since changes made in this window take effect immediately, you can try out the changes and see the results. Unless you want to open up more window space by removing the Button Menu or Status Line, there are not many changes you are likely to make on this menu.

The Confirmation Options window, shown in Figure 5.10, allows you to decide what actions require a Yes response before the program completes that task. Note that the default is all boxes checked. Once you become familiar with cc:Mail, you may want to turn off all these check boxes except `Confirm on delete`.

The `Fonts` choice on the Options menu allows you to change the fonts on some or all of your windows. With over ten window types and 12 fonts, the potential for creating messy screens certainly exists. The best use of this screen, shown in Figure 5.11, might be to select a larger-sized font to make the screen easier to read. You should note that the fonts you choose will not affect the text message area. You can't select a font and send a message featuring that font to someone else with cc:Mail for Windows.

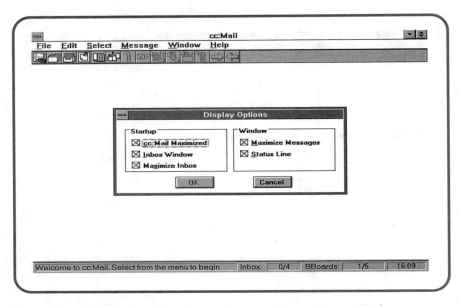

108

Figure 5.9   Check boxes used to configure the cc:Mail program and windows.

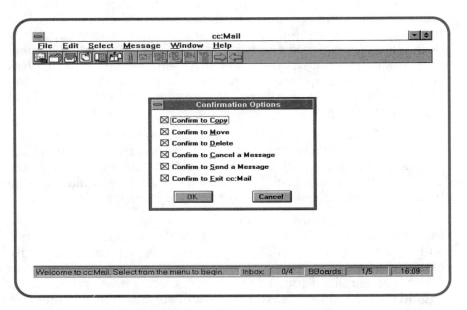

Figure 5.10   The Confirmation Options window.

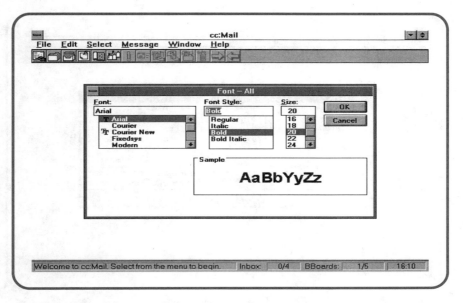

Figure 5.11 *The Fonts Dialog Box from the File Options menu choice.*

The Message Options allow you to designate the first item selected when you prepare a new message, set the default priority level, and make several other selections as shown in Figure 5.12. Notice that each row contains "radio buttons." Only one button at a time may be selected. By clicking on an open button, it fills in and the other button in the row opens up.

If you have cc:Mail running as an icon, it also checks your Inbox for messages. The Notify options provide several ways for the program to do this and specific intervals for the program to check as shown in Figure 5.13. When cc:Mail detects new mail, it can sound a tone and flash the icon or provide a dialog box, depending on your selections. Notice that you can use the check box next to Tone to turn it on or off. You can select either Notify Dialog or Flash Window for the visual reminder that new mail has arrived.

To change the default settings for the Inbox and Bulletin Board, move the cursor to that box and type the new setting. Five minutes for the Inbox provides quick responses to messages. If you have a large post office, the ten minute setting for the Bulletin Board may prove to be disruptive. Resetting this to 60 minutes may be frequent enough to know when new messages arrive on the Bulletin Board.

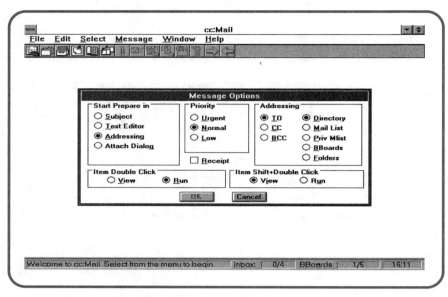

Figure 5.12 The Message Options Dialog Box.

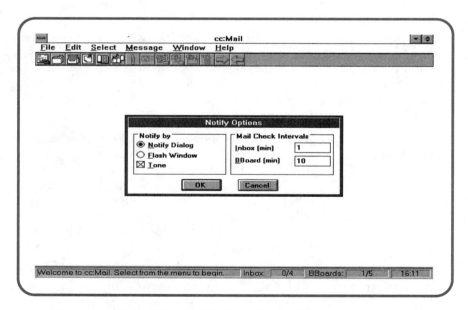

Figure 5.13 The Notify Options Dialog Box.

The List Options dialog box determines the order lists are displayed in the Inbox, Folders, Bulletin Boards and Archive files. These settings show the messages are "Last In" or "First In." The Last In setting shows the most recent items at the top of the list. The default setting has the Inbox and Bulletin Boards set as Last In and the Folders and Archives as First In.

The SmartIcons dialog box allows you to customize your cc:Mail screen. Icons on the strip (normally at the top of the screen) can be added or deleted and the strip itself can be positioned in different locations or can be removed completely. Figure 5.14 shows the first of two dialog boxes used to change the SmartIcons. The first setting allows the strip to be located on any of the four sides of the window or to float. The floating SmartIcon strip can be moved like a small window to any location on the screen. If the Show SmartIcon check mark is off, the icons will not appear on the screen and all functions must be accessed through the menus.

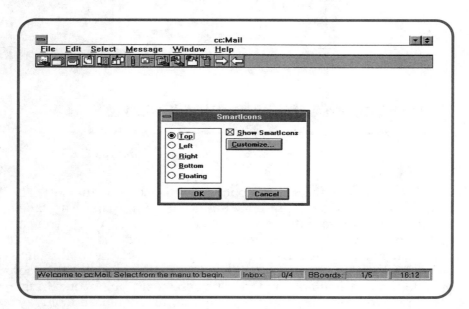

Figure 5.14   The first of two SmartIcons Dialog Boxes.

Clicking on the Customize button produces the dialog box shown in Figure 5.15. Any of the icons in the left box can be dragged to the right box. Point and click on any icon to see its description at the bottom of the window. All icons in the right box appear on the cc:Mail window. To remove an icon from the right box, drag it back to the left box.

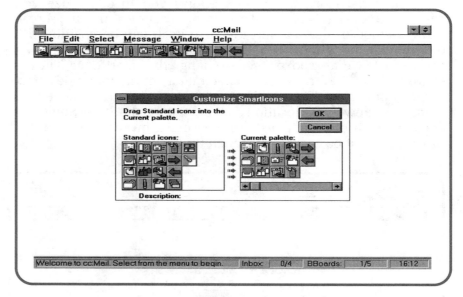

Figure 5.15   The Customize Dialog Box for SmartIcons.

For example, there are two icons with several mailboxes. The white mailbox icon represents Public Mailing Lists. The green mailbox icon represents your Private Mailing Lists. While you can open your private lists from Select on the menu bar, having this icon on the icon bar might save you time if you use private mailing lists a lot. By dragging this green mailbox icon to the right side, this icon would then be available on the main screen. To open your Private Mailing lists, you would just click on that newly placed icon.

Tip: The default settings for the SmartIcon bar does not include all the icons. You may want to create a more complete set of SmartIcons by dragging all the icons from the left box to the right box. You can easily remove some later if you find that you don't use them.

The Text Editor in cc:Mail for Windows can also be customized to your preferences. The Edit menu includes the Text Editor menu shown in Figure 5.16. From this menu, you can change the highlight colors (to make comments in someone else's message), set the margins and tabs, and toggle a ruler and paragraph formatting.

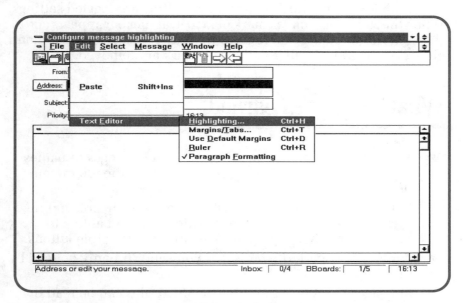

Figure 5.16   The Text Editor menu available in the Edit menu.

Some of these choices are only available if you are in the Text Editor. The most useful is the ability to change the highlight color. As noted in the DOS section, you can add your comments to a message in another color and then reply or forward the message item. This menu choice also allows you to change your default pen and background color.

 Tip: Combine the Color combinations with the fonts available under File Options Font to create more readable text.

113

The margins and tab settings can be set for your messages. If you make changes to the right or left margin, these affect only the current text message. If you want to make these the default settings for all your messages, may sure you click on the Save button before you select OK to close the dialog box.

Both the Ruler and Paragraph Formatting are toggled settings. When the Ruler has a check mark next to it, a ruler bar appears across the Text Editor screen. To remove that ruler, just select that menu choice again and the ruler and check mark are removed.

What You Have Learned

114

▶ You can create private mailing lists. Any changes to names in the post office directory are automatically made in your private lists.

▶ Public and private mailing lists make it easy to create unnecessary e-mail. Think carefully before you send a note to everyone in the company in five cities offering free kittens.

▶ For the most part, the messages you send can only be read by the recipients.

▶ Messages you save as archive or ASCII files can be read by anyone with access to those files.

▶ You can change your password, text colors, and margin settings in the Profile menu.

Chapter 6

Sending More Than Text

In This Chapter

► *Including DOS files*
► *Creating graphic items*
► *Attaching Snapshots*
► *Minding your e-mail manners*

A message is like a large envelope. Each message can contain just one text "letter" or up to 20 items. These items in the mail packet include text items you type, DOS files, graphic images, and fax files. Graphic files can be created with the Graphic Editor or with Snapshot. Fax files are available if your system administrator has installed the FaxView program on the network and if you have a graphics screen.

Attaching DOS Files

A message can have one or more DOS files attached as part of the message. These files can be either data files, which the receiver can translate back into the program format used to create them, or program files, which have the extensions COM, EXE, or BAT. The following Quick Steps create a message and attach a DOS file.

Attaching a DOS file

1. From the Main menu, select `Prepare new message`.

   The Address menu appears.

2. Select `Address to person` (or other type of address).

   Depending on the type of address you choose, a list of addresses, mailing lists, or bboards/folders appears.

3. Select the address or addresses for the message. Press Esc when finished.

   The Address menu returns with `eNd addressing` highlighted.

4. Press Enter or N.

   The cursor moves to the `Subject:` line.

5. Type a note about the contents of the message and press Enter.

   The cursor moves to the Message Contents area of the screen.

6. Type a message, probably describing the contents of the attached DOS file. Press F10 when finished.

   The Send menu appears with `Send message` highlighted.

7. Select `attach copy of dos File`.

   The current subdirectory containing the Mail program appears.

8. Backspace to clear the line. Then type the drive, directory, and DOS filename to attach and press Enter.

   The Send menu reappears. The screen will show a 1 next to the text item and a 2 next to the file item.

9. Continue to attach items until you've completed the message. Press Enter or S to send the message.

   After the message is sent, the Main menu appears.

□

The cc:Mail screen for attaching a file can be used several ways. The program assumes that the file you want to attach is in the current directory at the time you started Mail. Figure 6.1 shows the current directory immediately after selecting attach copy of dos File from the Send menu.

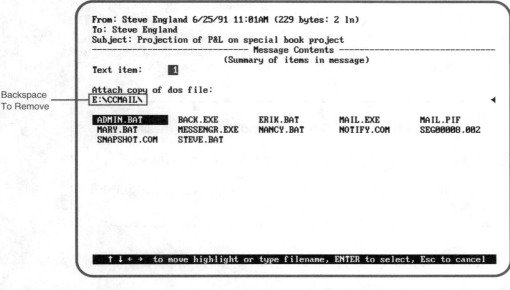

Backspace
To Remove

```
From: Steve England 6/25/91 11:01AM (229 bytes: 2 ln)
To: Steve England
Subject: Projection of P&L on special book project
------------------------------ Message Contents ------------------------------
                    (Summary of items in message)

Text item:        1

Attach copy of dos file:
E:\CCMAIL\                                                                    ◄

 ADMIN.BAT        BACK.EXE        ERIK.BAT        MAIL.EXE        MAIL.PIF
 MARY.BAT         MESSENGR.EXE    NANCY.BAT       NOTIFY.COM      SEG00008.002
 SNAPSHOT.COM     STEVE.BAT




 ↑ ↓ ← →  to move highlight or type filename, ENTER to select, Esc to cancel
```

**Figure 6.1   *The current directory for attaching a copy of a DOS
file to a message.***

117

You can use the Arrow keys to move around this list of files, or
you can begin typing and have cc:Mail narrow down the choice of
files. You cannot change drives or directories without first using
Backspace to remove the current drive and path. As you backspace
over the directory, cc:Mail will redisplay files or directories. As you
remove the drive letter, in this case the E: drive, the program returns
to the original directory listing. If you type a new drive designation,
cc:Mail again shifts the display.

This constant shifting may be confusing. Provided you know
the exact drive and directory of the DOS file, you can just type the
entire line. For example, if you have a subdirectory called SHEETS
on drive C: and a filename of P&L.WQ1, you would backspace to
delete the current line and then, at the attach copy of dos file
prompt, type C:\SHEETS\P&L.WQ1.

> **Tip:** Remember that the DOS file attached to the message
> is only a copy of the original file. Therefore, any changes
> you make to the original file will not affect the file attached to
> the message.

Attaching a DOS file is not the same as reading a text file into a message. When a file is included in the text message with Alt-F9, you can use the Editor program to make changes. However, you cannot change an attached DOS file from within cc:Mail. For more information on loading text files into messages, see Chapter 3, "Sending Mail."

 What kinds of DOS files do you attach to messages?

All kinds, especially documents for use by the field staff.

Generally application data files, that is, spreadsheets, graphic files, etc.

118

Inserting Graphic Items

Messages can also include graphic images. Each image is attached to a message as an item, which is displayed on one screen. Graphic images can be produced either with cc:Mail's Graphic Editor or with Snapshot, both of which are covered in Chapter 7, "Special Features and Programs."

All graphic items are displayed on the Inbox message list with a g for graphic. A finished graphic item may be reedited by pressing an Arrow key while viewing the item. This will return you to the Graphic Editor. Once created, they cannot be edited or changed. In order to attach a graphic item or a Snapshot file, you need to follow two different procedures, as outlined in the next two sets of Quick Steps.

 Attaching a graphic item

1. After addressing and preparing your text for the first item of the message, press F10.

   The Send menu appears with the highlight on attach copy of dos File.

2. Select attach new iTems.

   The Attach menu appears with attach Text item highlighted.

3. Select `attach Graphics item`.   The Graphic Editor screen appears.

4. Create the graphic item you want to send. Press F1 for help. Press F10 when done. (See Chapter 7 for more information.)   The `Item title` prompt appears.

5. Type a descriptive title of the graphic drawing just created. Press Enter when done.   The Attach menu appears.

6. Select `eNd attaching`.   The Send menu reappears with the highlight on `Send message`.

7. Press Enter or S to send the message.   The Main menu appears. □

These Quick Steps leave out the process of creating the graphic image with the Graphic Editor, which is covered in Chapter 7. You should note that movement of the drawing tool in the Graphic Editor is limited to the keyboard. Although you can use a mouse (which requires special mouse software), it can only duplicate keystrokes.

You might find it more useful to send graphic images by combining your favorite graphics software and the Snapshot program supplied with cc:Mail. With Snapshot you can create the screen image and then capture it in a format cc:Mail can display. More information about using Snapshot is included in Chapter 7. These Quick Steps cover the process of inserting a Snapshot file as a message item.

119

Q Attaching a Snapshot file

1. After addressing and preparing your text for the first item of the message, press F10.   The Send menu appears with the highlight on `attach copy of dos File`.

2. Select `attach new iTems`.   The Attach menu appears with `attach Text item` highlighted.

3. Select `attach Snapshots`.   The current subdirectory containing the Mail program appears.

4. Backspace to clear the line. Then type the drive, directory, and Snapshot filename to attach and press Enter.	The graphic image appears on the screen.
5. Press Enter.	The Item title prompt appears.
6. Type a descriptive title of the screen image. Press Enter when done.	The latest directory appears.
7. Continue to attach Snapshot files. Press Esc when complete.	The Attach menu appears with the highlight on attach Text item.
8. Select eNd attaching.	The Send menu appears with Send message highlighted.
9. Continue to attach items using the attach new iTems choice or press Enter or S to send the message.	After the message is sent, the Main menu appears.

120

☐

Because a Snapshot file can only be viewed in cc:Mail, it must be attached as a graphic item. This process is similar to that used when attaching a DOS file, except that cc:Mail checks the graphic file before attaching it to the message and then shows you the attached file. If the file is not a Snapshot file, cc:Mail provides an error message and allows you to try again.

> **Tip:** Once attached to a message, a Snaphot may be edited in the Graphic Editor by pressing an Arrow key while viewing the Snapshot.

Including Bulletin Board and Folder Items

Messages saved in your private folders and on the public bulletin boards can also be attached to a message you are preparing. However, you must first know their message numbers before you begin preparing the message. The following Quick Steps assume you have reviewed the contents of a folder and want to attach several messages as items to the message you are composing.

Q Attaching a bulletin board or folder message

1. After addressing and preparing your text for the first
   item of the message, press F10.

   The Send menu appears
   with the highlight on
   attach copy of dos File.

2. Select attach new iTems.

   The Attach menu appears
   with attach Text item
   highlighted.

3. Select attach bboard
   /folder Msgs.

   A list of bulletin
   boards/folders appears.

4. Select the bulletin board or
   folder name containing the
   messages you want to use
   and press Enter.

   The prompt Attach msg
   numbers appears.

5. Type the message numbers,
   separated by a space. Press
   Enter.

   Each item appears on the
   screen after you press Enter.
   The Attach menu appears.

6. Continue to attach items. To
   finish, select eNd attaching.

   The Send menu appears
   with Send message highlighted.

7. Press Enter or S to send
   the message.

   After the message is sent,
   the Main menu appears. □

121

As noted, attaching message items from your folder or the bulletin boards takes some preparation. Once you have attached the items, you see them in the order that they were attached.

> **Tip:** If you are attaching more than two or three messages, you may first want to create a temporary folder and copy the messages from other folders and bulletin boards to that temporary folder. Then you can enter the message numbers from that temporary folder in the order you want the receiver to view the items.

E-Mail Etiquette

Your e-mail messages convey more than just words or images. They also suggest a lot about you, the author of the message. The message structure, the spelling, and the clarity of the thoughts are all part of the message. Watching how others use the system and spending time developing your own manners will help your messages convey exactly what you intend.

Work groups vary a great deal in their approach to sending e-mail messages. Some groups retain the formality of written communications. Their messages could easily be printed and sent as memos, and there would be no evidence that these memos started as e-mail. Such messages can be read two months later, and the meaning will still be quite clear.

Other groups use e-mail as though everyone is in the middle of an on-going discussion. These messages make sense only when they are read in order. They often have missing punctuation and haphazard spelling and are likely to contain extra expressions, such as <grin> and <frown>, that convey emotional reactions. Such messages usually lose their meaning or significance in only a few days.

The most effective use of e-mail falls within these two extremes. A formal message system requires more time to compose a message, which is likely to limit the number of messages exchanged. An extremely informal system is transitory and may end up being used only as a supplement to telephone tag.

Common E-Mail "Rules"

E-Mail etiquette is neither complex nor confusing but consists of a few common rules, which are discussed in the following paragraphs.

Messages usually do not contain a salutation or closing. This may be because the address lines show both the sender and receiver. Some users develop a "signature" phrase for the end of their message, such as "Later..." or "Another glowing thought." Such "cute" closings can end up being equivalent to "From the desk of" note pads.

A forwarded message should acknowledge the thoughts of the original author. If one or more people contribute to a message, each additional author should use the cc:Mail highlight feature to show his or her contribution. The beginning of the message can contain a small line, in the author's highlight, showing his or her name and the date of additions.

Insert the answers to the questions right in the original message. The cc:Mail reply feature is very useful for responses to specific questions. Use the highlight to make these responses stand out.

If you don't use the original message in the response, at least summarize the discussion in the opening sentence. A response to a message like "I agree with that idea" provides the receiver with no clue about the original discussion. The receiver may be having several different e-mail discussions at the same time. Expand the message to: "I agree with your plan to expand the art department. Let's go with your ideas."

Before you send a message to a large mailing list, consider how important the message is to everyone. If it's not essential that everyone see the message, you should post it on a bulletin board instead.

123

Don't be reluctant to use e-mail because you worry about proper punctuation. Keep your sentences short. Don't try to get fancy. End each sentence with a period or question mark. Remember that most readers won't worry about an occasional misplaced comma. Leave that to the professional editors.

Don't refuse to send messages just because you're a poor speller. Few people are willing to admit they can't spell well, and with e-mail your mistakes are exposed to the world. However, you can use several approaches to overcome this problem:

1. You can compose messages with a word processor equipped with a spell checker. After spell-checking your messages, you can load them into the cc:Mail Editor program or send them as attached text files.

2. You can use special programs that check the spelling of any word on the screen, including the cc:Mail Editor program. These programs can watch as you type, signal a misspelled word, and offer suggested corrections.

3. You can just misspell words to your heart's content. Your unique spelling will be seen as part of you, just like your wild ties, polished loafers, or perfume.

4. If you are afraid that you look too silly, you can at least admit that you don't know how to spell a word. Just add (sp?) after the word. Then the reader will know that you're unsure about the word's spelling.

DON'T SHOUT UNLESS YOU MEAN IT. Some people claim they save time by turning on the Caps Lock key because they don't want to capitalize words properly. However, a message that is entirely capitalized suggests shouting. SAVE THE SHOUTING FOR WHEN YOU MEAN IT.

The other extreme from shouting is no capitalization at all. This style may not include punctuation either—this is laid back—casual conversation—it also may suggest a rather random process—cool if it works for you—hope your reader is cool too.

You can include emotional hints to enhance the content of a message. For example, you can write <grin> at the end of a sarcastic or teasing statement or use a worried look to convey concern. The < and > characters emphasize the emotional nature of the word. These emotional punctuation marks can also be rather cryptic. Various combinations of characters provide different meanings. Take these, for example: :) ;) 8-) :<. Viewed with your head turned 90 degrees to the left, these characters represent a smile, a wink, a smiling face with glasses, and a big frown. But be careful. You can spend as much time creating cute faces as writing the message. Of course, you can also use the ASCII grin characters by holding down the Alt Key and pressing 1 or 2 on the numeric keypad.

Respond as quickly as possible to a message. If you can't supply a complete response, at least let the sender know that you are working on the response and that you think you can send it by a certain date. Then stick to that promised date.

Never write something about someone else that you wouldn't want them or others to read. If you must be critical, provide specific incidents on which you formed your opinion. If you intend for the message to remain private, state that clearly in the message.

Remember that a mild complaint appears more serious when written down. Unless you have specific suggestions for resolving the situation, don't commit the complaint to writing. You'll just waste everyone's time.

Ask yourself what you want to convey. If you want to get three points across, type those first on the screen. Then use Editor in the insert mode to expand each point into a paragraph. If you want to make doubly sure the reader understands what you're emphasizing, you can summarize each idea in a sentence at the end of the message.

Keep critical copies of messages in folders or archive files.
Make sure the Subject: line contains enough information to help
you find that message again if necessary.

> **Tip:** Electronic mail presents a new way to capture and
> convey thoughts. Thinking about the potential impact of
> the message on one or more readers is the first and best way to
> use this channel of communications effectively.

> **What irritates you about e-mail messages? What do you
> appreciate?**
>
> I like that they tend to be better thought out and clearer than
> most phone conversations or phone mail.
>
> Guaranteed e-mail is currently the thorn in my side. For
> example, how can I maintain personal mail security and still
> print and mail a hard copy if the user hasn't read his or her mail
> in x days?

125

For Windows Users

The Windows Attach (paper clip) icon allows you to attach additional text files, DOS files, and graphic images. You can attach items
at any point while completing a message by clicking on the Attach
icon. Figure 6.2 shows the Message Item Attachment window,
which is accessed through this icon.

To attach a DOS file to the message, select the file from the list
in the Files box. You can click on a different drive if you want to
change drives. Likewise, you can click on subdirectory names to
move into that directory and on the parent directory (.) to move up
a level. Once you have located the file to attach, click on that
filename. The Files box now contains that filename. Click on the OK
button, and the file is copied to that message. A new icon is then
placed in the Message Item area signifying the attached DOS file.

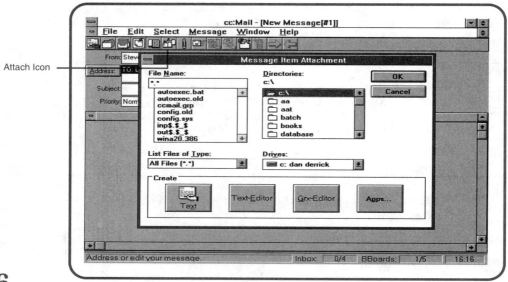

Attach Icon

Figure 6.2   The Message Item Attachment window.

The bottom of the Message Item Attachment window also contains several buttons that you can use to attach items to a message. Selecting the Text button returns you to the cc:Mail Editor program to create another text item. This would be useful if you wanted to comment on another message without making changes to the first. Comments added to a text item will therefore appear as part of the original text. You can also use the Text button to create a small presentation with graphic items and text items interspersed in the message. The receiver could then read an explanation of each graphic item immediately after viewing the image.

The Text-Editor button allows you to use a different editor to create the text messages. The cc:Mail installation program automatically uses the Windows Notepad program as the alternative editor. This option provides two advantages: you can work in a word processing program you already know how to use, and you can create a template file to load automatically into this word processor. Figure 6.3 shows the results of starting the Text-Editor, which automatically loaded the template file TEMPLATE.SAM.

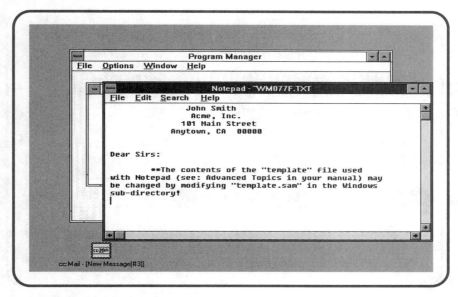

Figure 6.3   The Notepad program started from the Message Item Attachment window.

127

If you use the Text-Editor button to create additional text items, you may want to change the default text editor. You will definitely want to create a new template file. For information on setting up a different Windows text editor, consult your system administrator, who can refer to the "Advanced Topics" section of the cc:Mail for Windows *User's Manual*.

The Grx-Editor button automatically starts the Windows Paintbrush program. The filenames are assigned automatically by cc:Mail. You can also substitute another graphics program by modifying the WIN.INI file. Again, for further details, check with your system administrator.

The Apps... button opens another window to attach a new file as shown in Figure 6.4. The installation program installs Write, PC Paintbrush, and Notepad. Notice that the Notepad and Paintbrush programs are also available from the previous window. These are likewise installed with the WIN.INI file.

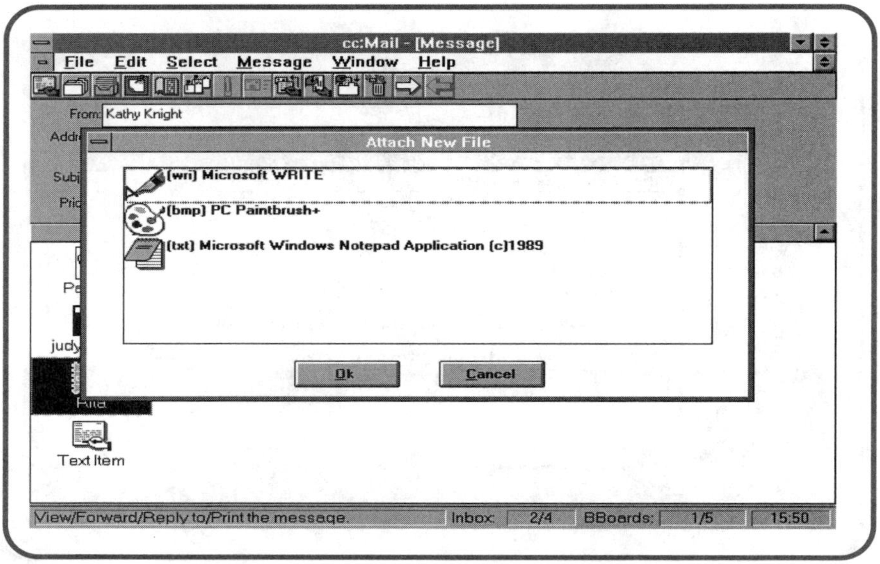

Figure 6.4   The additional applications available from the
Attach icon.

The current version of cc:Mail for Windows also allows you to copy a message from your current folder or from a bulletin board to a message being prepared. To do so, open the existing message and drag each item from the old message into the Message items box of the new message.

What You Have Learned

► Messages contain items consisting of text, DOS files, graphic screens, and fax files.

► When a DOS file is attached to a message, only a copy of that file is sent along with the message.

► Graphic items can be created with the built-in cc:Mail Graphic Editor program or with the external Snapshot program. They can then be attached as items to a message.

▶ Folder and bulletin board messages can also be attached to a message, but you must first know the message number before you can prepare the message.

▶ Like any human interaction, e-mail messages communicate with their appearance as well as content. Take time to consider the recipient or recipients of the message and the entire appearance of your message.

▶ The Windows version of cc:Mail does not allow messages to be easily copied from folders and bulletin boards to new messages.

Special Features and Programs

In This Chapter

▶ *Receiving timely notification of new messages*
▶ *Reading and responding while in other programs*
▶ *Creating and editing graphic images*
▶ *Capturing screen images from other programs*

Two cc:Mail programs included in the cc:Mail software package can notify you when mail has arrived in your mailbox and can read and send mail from within other programs. These programs, Notify and Messenger, are located in the subdirectory containing the MAIL.EXE program. Both programs are run from the DOS prompt and can continue working while you are using other DOS programs.

The cc:Mail Snapshot program, also located in the same subdirectory, allows you to capture screens from other programs to send as a message item. This program, along with the Graphic Editor program, allows you to send graphic items with your messages.

Mail in Your Box: Notify

The Notify program in cc:Mail can run in background, or *resident*, mode while you use other programs. It checks at specified intervals to see if you have any new messages in your mailbox. If you do, the program provides a small window on the screen and a tone. You can also check your Inbox status at any time by pressing the hotkey combination Alt-2.

Loading Notify in the resident mode is similar to loading the Mail program. You enter the program name, your name, and the drive and directory with the cc:Mail post office. For example, you might type:

```
M:CCMAIL\>NOTIFY STEVE ENGLAND M:\CCDATA
```

132

Notice that the password is not necessary on this command line, since this program does not access your messages. You may also start the program by typing **NOTIFY**. In this case, as when you start Mail, the program prompts you for each piece of information before running. When first run, the program checks your mailbox and reports the number of messages, as shown in Figure 7.1.

 Do you use Notify?

Yes. It's an important part of responding quickly to those who need my help.

Yes, we use Notify, but not in resident mode. It is run as part of our log-on sequence to notify users if they have any mail waiting.

Yes. That way we have immediate feedback in case of an urgent message.

```
M:\CCMAIL>NOTIFY STEVE ENGLAND M:\CCDATA
Version 3.20  Copyright (c) 1991.  cc:Mail, Inc.  All rights reserved.
cc:Mail NOTIFY installed for Steve England.  New message key is Alt2.
4 new Inbox messages
2 new Bulletin Board messages

M:\CCMAIL>NOTIFY REMOVE
cc:Mail NOTIFY will be removed from memory.

M:\CCMAIL>NOTIFY STEVE ENGLAND M:\CCDATA HEADINGS
Password: ▓▓▓▓
Version 3.20  Copyright (c) 1991.  cc:Mail, Inc.  All rights reserved.
cc:Mail NOTIFY installed for Steve England.  New message key is Alt2.
4 new Inbox messages
2 new Bulletin Board messages

    cc:Fax                  7/20/91  2302t    Fax send ERROR for 7/15/91 4:31PM m
    cc:Fax                  7/20/91  2264t    Fax send ERROR for 7/15/91 2:39PM m
    Administrator at FAX 7/20/91  14240x   Message not deliverable
    Steve England          6/28/91  159t     Double up

M:\CCMAIL>
```

Figure 7.1   The Response screen message when Notify is first run.

133

Notify Command Lines

You can use Notify to check your mailbox without loading it into memory, and the program will report the number of new Inbox and bulletin board messages. You can also quickly check the new message headers in your Inbox and even automatically start Mail with Notify. In short, the Notify program can be used in several different ways with different command lines, as the following examples illustrate. (Note that M:\CCDATA is used in place of your actual post office address.)

NOTIFY *first last* **M:\CCDATA CHKONLY**

You use the CHKONLY parameter just to check your Inbox. In this case, Notify does not load into memory.

NOTIFY *first last $us password* **M:\CCDATA HEADINGS**

The HEADINGS parameter displays the Inbox list of new messages when you first start Notify or when you press the hotkey combination Alt-2. Notice the need for the password in the command line.

NOTIFY *first last password* **M:\CCDATA HEADINGS CHKONLY**

You can combine the HEADINGS and CHKONLY parameters to get a quick list of the message subjects without loading Notify permanently.

NOTIFY REMOVE

This removes the resident copy of Notify from memory. Be careful, though. If other programs have been loaded after Notify, problems might occur after removing this program from memory.

NOTIFY *first last* **M:\CCDATA ALT0**

This changes the hotkey combination from the default of Alt-2 to Alt-0. The letters a to z and A to Z as well as ! @ # $ % ^ & * ( ) - _ = + may be used with the Alt key. Notice that lowercase "a" is not the same as "A." If the uppercase "A" is used, the hotkey combination would be Alt-Shift-A. If the "$" is used, the hotkey combination would be Alt-Shift-4.

NOTIFY *first last* **M:\CCDATA CLEAR/0**

The CLEAR parameter with a 0 leaves the message window on the screen until you press the Esc key. To set the number of seconds the window remains on the screen, use a number up to 3600 (60 minutes). The default for the screen to clear is five seconds.

NOTIFY *first last* **M:\CCDATA TIMER/15**

The interval used to check your mailbox is set with the TIMER parameter. This example changes the interval to every 15 minutes instead of the standard 5 minutes. A value of 0 keeps Notify from checking automatically. In this case, Notify checks for new messages only when the hotkey combination is used.

With all these options, you may find it difficult to determine the best way to use Notify. The following series of questions helps you decide what to include on the command line. Once you've chosen the best command line for your needs, the Quick Steps show you how to create a quick way to use this command line in a batch file.

1. Do you want Notify to inform you of new messages when you are in other programs? If not, add **CHKONLY** to the command line.

2. Do you want to see the message headings? If yes, add **HEADINGS** to the command line and include your password.

3. Do you want to have the Notice window remain on the screen until you press Esc? If yes, add **CLEAR/0** to the command line.

4. Do you want Notify to check for new messages more or less frequently than every five minutes? If yes, add **TIMER/#** to the command line where # equals from 1 to 3600 (60 minutes).

5. Do you want Notify to check for messages only when you use the hotkey combination? If yes, add **TIMER/0** to the command line.

6. Do you want to use a different key with the Alt key for the hotkey combination? If yes, add **ALT*** to the command line where * represents a different letter or number.

135

> **Tip:** If you try to load Notify again with another command line option, you get a warning message to remove current NOTIFY first. Use **NOTIFY REMOVE**. Then try another command line option.

Using Notify in Batch Files

Once you have tested the command, you can create a small batch file to make the process even quicker. Remember, you don't need to use this method to access Notify, but it is more convenient. Make sure you are in your root directory before you start these Quick Steps. The system prompt should be C:\.

For these Quick Steps, the example line is:

NOTIFY STEVE ENGLAND *password* **M:\CCDATA HEADINGS TIMER/10 CLEAR/0**

Q Creating a batch file for Notify

1. Type **COPY CON: CHKMAIL.BAT** and press Enter.	The DOS prompt disappears.
2. Type the drive letter containing the cc:Mail program and a colon. Press Enter.	The cursor moves to the next line.
3. Type the following, substituting a different subdirectory name if necessary: **CD \CCMAIL** Press Enter.	The cursor moves to the next line.
4. Type the following on one line only, substituting your name for STEVE ENGLAND and your post office address for **M:\CCDATA**: **NOTIFY STEVE ENGLAND %1 M:\CCDATA HEADINGS TIMER/10 CLEAR/0** Press Enter.	The cursor moves to the next line.
5. Press F6.	DOS responds with `1 File(s) copied.`
6. To test this batch file, type **CHKMAIL** and your password separated by a space.	The Notify program runs as instructed in the command. □

136

In the command line above you used **% 1** in place of your password. The batch file will then substitute the password you enter when CHKMAIL starts the Notify program. This provides a quick way to start cc:Mail and still protects your password. If you are not using the HEADINGS parameter, you do not need to include your password.

A more advanced use of Notify and batch files allows Notify to run the Mail program automatically. To do so, simply insert the following lines in your AUTOEXEC.BAT file, substituting names and directories as appropriate. (Note that you can still use all the Notify parameters available on the first line.)

```
M:\CCMAIL\NOTIFY STEVE ENGLAND M:\CCDATA
IF ERRORLEVEL 1 MAIL STEVE ENGLAND M:\CCDATA
```

Now when you boot the system, the first line runs the Notify program. If there are any messages in your Inbox, Notify returns a DOS error code number corresponding to the number of new messages. Although this number does not represent an actual error, it is read in the batch file as the variable ERRORLEVEL, which is then tested by the IF statement. Once you have completed the Mail session, Notify remains in effect, depending on the parameters in that line of the batch file.

From within Other Programs: Messenger

The cc:Mail Messenger program combines several functions contained in both Notify and Mail. It checks your mailbox and notifies you when a new message has arrived in your mailbox. You can then immediately read and respond to messages from within the current DOS program.

> **Caution:** Because Messenger uses memory, you may find that some programs requiring a lot of memory no longer run after Messenger has been loaded. You may not be able to use Messenger and those programs simultaneously. In this case, use **MESSENGR REMOVE** to free up memory.

Because Messenger must conserve memory, a number of features in Mail are not available. The significant limitations include:

► Help is not available through the F1 key.
► You can't manage your mailbox or change your profile.
► You can't use highlighting in the program's editor.
► You can't address to a mailing list or send to more than 20 mailboxes at one time.

► You must know the name of a folder to which you want to copy (but not move) a message.

► You can't use the Graphic Editor or attach Snapshots.

► You can edit only one screen of text.

► You cannot import other text files into a message.

► You can read only the first 22 messages in your Inbox.

► Messenger may not work from within some graphics programs.

Like the Mail program, Messenger is started from the DOS prompt. You type the program name **MESSENGR** (notice the missing "e"), and the program prompts for your name, password, and post office location. You can also include all this information on the command line, since Messenger uses many of the parameters available in Notify, including REMOVE, CLEAR, ALT, TIMER, and, additionally, PASSWORD.

138

Once Messenger is loaded into memory, pressing the hotkey combination opens your mailbox. This leaves your mail open to anyone with access to your keyboard. The PASSWORD parameter prompts you for your password when you use the hotkey combination to call up the Messenger window.

The Main menu in Messenger, shown in Figure 7.2, provides two choices: Read inbox messages and Prepare new message. Once a selection has been made, the process of creating or reading a message is similar to that in Mail. Some menu choices are not available based on the limitations noted above.

The PASSWORD parameter in the command line provides a prompt each time you call up Messenger with the hotkey combination. A sample command line would be:

MESSENGR STEVE ENGLAND PASSWORD M:\CCDATA

If you mistype the password at the prompt, an error window appears, and you are returned to the original program. Use the hotkey combination to try again.

Messenger provides the convenience of reading and responding to messages quickly without leaving your current program. Its limitations prevent you from creating graphics or text items more than one page long. If you want to save the message to a folder, you need to know and type the entire name of a folder in your mailbox. The list of folders is not displayed. If the folder does not exist, you can keep trying until you find it.

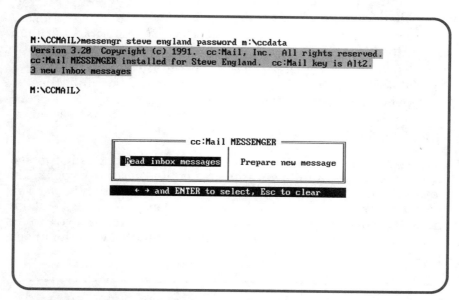

```
M:\CCMAIL>messengr steve england password m:\ccdata
Version 3.20  Copyright (c) 1991.  cc:Mail, Inc.  All rights reserved.
cc:Mail MESSENGER installed for Steve England.  cc:Mail key is Alt2.
3 new Inbox messages

M:\CCMAIL>
```

```
┌──────────────── cc:Mail MESSENGER ────────────────┐
│ ┌─────────────────────┐                           │
│ │ Read inbox messages │   Prepare new message     │
│ └─────────────────────┘                           │
├───────────────────────────────────────────────────┤
│    ← → and ENTER to select, Esc to clear          │
└───────────────────────────────────────────────────┘
```

Figure 7.2   The Messenger Main menu.

139

Getting Graphic: The Graphic Editor

In addition to a text editor, cc:Mail contains a graphic editor. This is not a separate program like Notify and Messenger, but is loaded from the Attach menu by selecting attach Graphics item. The Graphic Editor is available only if you have a graphics screen.

The Graphic Editor is limited to one screen and does not use a mouse at all. But the combination of Arrow keys for cursor movement and menu shortcut keys can be useful for making notes on screens originally captured with Snapshot. (Chapter 6, "Sending More Than Text," provides the specific steps for attaching a graphic image to a message.)

You can initiate the Graphic Editor in one of three ways:

▶ To create a new graphic image, select attach Graphics item from the Attach menu. This starts the Graphic Editor with a blank screen.

▶ To edit a Snapshot image, select attach Snapshots from the Attach menu. This loads a Snapshot image on the screen. Then press F9 to load the Graphic Editor.

▶ To edit a graphic image, select display Message from the Send menu, which brings up the Action menu. Then select display Item to display a graphic image you have created. Then press F9 to load the Graphic Editor.

Figure 7.3 shows the initial screen for a new graphic image, which you create by following the first method described above. The lower right corner contains the tool and color selection icons. This part of the screen can be displayed or hidden by pressing F9 at any time. Pressing F10 saves the graphic image and returns you to the Send menu. To exit the Graphic Editor without saving the image, press Esc.

140

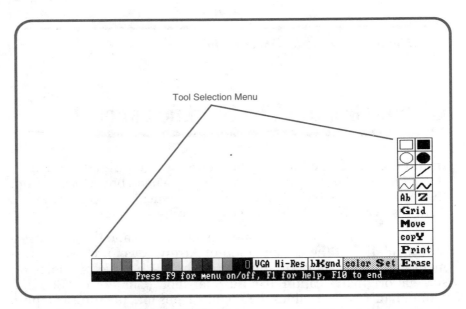

Figure 7.3   The Tool Selection menu available when creating a new graphic image from the Attach menu.

The Arrow keys move the cursor around on the screen eight positions, or *pixels*, at a time. To restrict movement to one position at a time, hold down on the Shift key while pressing the Arrow keys. The Home, End, PgUp, and PgDn keys move the cursor to the corner of the screen that corresponds to the key's position on the keyboard. For example, the Home key is in the upper left corner relative to the other three keys, so Home moves the cursor to the upper left corner of the screen.

Tools

When the Tool Selection menu is active, you can select any tools by moving the highlight with the Arrow keys and pressing Enter. Each tool also has a special selection key, called a *Power Key*, as noted in Figure 7.4. Once a tool has been selected, the menu disappears from the screen. The menu can be recalled at any time with the F9 key.

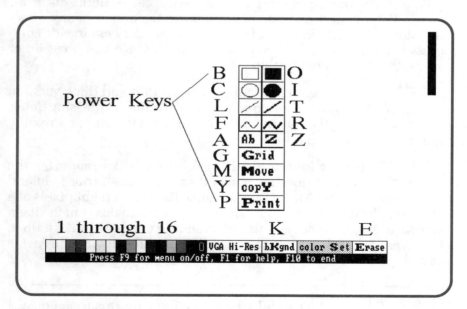

Figure 7.4   The Power Keys for each tool.

The first six tools allow you to draw on the screen. These consist of the open and filled box, the open and filled circle, the thin and thick line, and the thin and thick freehand line. They all work with a combination of Arrow keys and Enter. Drawing an image involves four basic steps:

1. Move the cursor to the location for the image.
2. Press Enter to start creating the image.
3. Use the Arrow keys to create the image.
4. Press Enter again to finish the image.

Once you press Enter a second time, the image you have created becomes permanent. You must use the Erase tool to remove all or parts of that image.

The open and filled boxes are created the same way. Place the cursor where you want one corner of a square or rectangle. Then press Enter to place that corner. Use the Arrow keys to expand the image to the size you want. Press Enter again to complete the box. If you selected the Filled Box tool, the rectangle is filled in as soon as you press Enter. You can continue to use this tool or press F9 to return to the Tool and Color Selection menu.

142

The open and filled circles use the center of the circle for their starting point. As you move the cursor in any direction after pressing Enter the first time, cross hairs enlarge or compress to show the size of the resulting circle. Once you press Enter again, the circle is completed.

The Straight Line tool provides a thin and thick version. Once you place one end point of the line by pressing Enter, you can "stretch" the line in any direction with the cursor. Pressing Enter again places that line.

The Drawing tool also has a thin and thick version, but the tool itself does not make it easy to create true freehand lines. Normally the Arrow keys advance the cursor eight pixels at a time, resulting in a line that consists of right angles, much like a staircase. You can reduce this movement to one position at a time, however, by holding down on the Shift key while moving the Arrow keys.

Caution: Be careful when drawing with this tool. Once active, any movement adds to the image. Accidentally pressing Home, End, PgDn, or PgUp moves the cursor to a corner, leaving behind a trail as it moves.

Ab Z The two Text tools allow you to use two different sizes of text. The smaller text provides 80 characters across the screen, whereas the larger text provides 40 characters.

To insert text in the graphic image, place the cursor where you want to position the text and begin typing. Notice that several keys do not have the same functions in these Text tools as in a word processor. For example, the Enter key moves the cursor just below the original starting point. The Backspace key deletes a letter but does not move the text to close up the resulting blank space. And the Del and Ins keys do not work.

Grid The Grid tool provides reference points on the screen. Selecting Grid the first time displays points 16 pixels apart. Selecting Grid again removes these reference points. Like the lines on graph paper, these points can be used to help align parts of your image.

Move

copY Both the Move and Copy tools allow you to select a part of the image and move or copy it to another part of the screen. You start by positioning the cursor at one corner of the area you want to move or copy and press Enter. Then move the cursor until you've defined this area and press Enter again. Lines appear on the screen to show the position of the first corner marked. Use the Arrow keys to move the selected area to a new location.

Once you press Enter, the image is "pasted" over the current image. If you selected Move, the original section is missing. If you selected Copy, the original remains in the starting position.

Print The Print tool is a menu choice to print the image to a graphics printer. The Graphic Editor uses the printer setting in the Profile menu. If you do not have a graphics printer, this icon will have a gray background, indicating that you cannot make this selection.

Erase The Erase icon allows you to remove parts of the image. This selection returns the image color to the background color. Once selected, Erase is used like Move and Copy, except that the image contained in the marked box is erased.

color Set The Color Set icon is available only with CGA screens. Selecting this icon cycles you through the four color combinations available with that screen type. If you have an EGA or VGA screen, there is little reason to select the lower CGA

143

resolution. cc:Mail translates images if necessary from higher (VGA/EGA) to lower screen resolutions. For example, if you create an image on a VGA screen and send the item to someone with a CGA screen, cc:Mail translates the image as accurately as possible.

| bKgnd | The Background icon (bKgnd) cycles through the possible colors for the image background. On EGA and VGA screens, this selection can be one of 16 colors. When the background color matches a color on the screen, that image color shifts to another color. In most cases, the best background colors are blue, black, white, or gray.

| VGA Hi-Res | Before you begin drawing, you can select the resolution with this icon. The icon name changes as you cycle through with the Enter key. Once you have begun creating an image, this icon locks on that current resolution. If you select the CGA Lo-Res screen type, the Color Set icon is active. You can change the basic four colors only with the CGA screen.

In addition to text and line, color may differ for each part of an image. To select the color for part of the image, move the Highlight box to the color you want and press Enter. A small square inside the color box marks the current drawing color.

The number of colors available varies with the type of screen. CGA Hi-Res and Herc are limited to black and white. CGA Lo-Res can contain four colors selected from four possible combinations with the Color Set icon. EGA and VGA screens all have 16 colors. A drawing created with colors can still be viewed on the lower resolution screen, but the colors are not present.

Drawing

Learning to draw a graphic image with any graphics program is mostly a matter of trial and error. When first learning, don't attempt to create a specific image. Just select and try out each tool on the menu. Practice several times with each one. After you become familiar with the capabilities of each tool, you will be ready to attempt a meaningful image.

Modifying Snapshots

Probably the most useful way to use the Graphic Editor is to make notes on screens captured with Snapshot. Once you have selected the Snapshot to attach (a process explained in Chapter 6), that image is displayed on the screen. Press F9 to show the Graphic Editor's Tool icons. You can then make changes and additions to that image using those tools.

A slightly more advanced method is to use another graphics editor to create the graphic image to attach to your message. You load the Snapshot program (explained in the next section), create the image in your own graphics editor, and then capture that image with the Snapshot program. Figures 7.5 and 7.6 show the process of creating that image and the resulting screen image in the message.

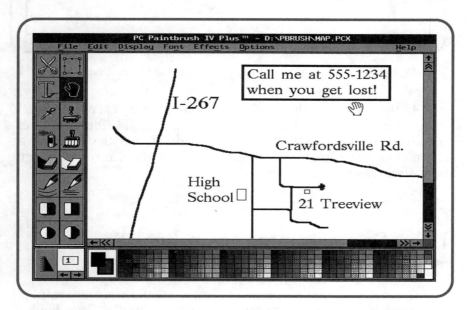

Figure 7.5   A graphic image created with PC Paintbrush IV Plus.

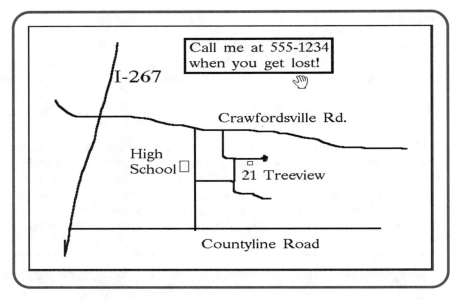

Figure 7.6 *The final screen image captured with Snapshot.*

146

In this example, the image was created with PC Paintbrush IV Plus. This graphics program has a number of additional features, including mouse control and Edit Undo. Once the image was completed, the screen was cleared to show the entire image and Snapshot was called up with Alt-1.

Using Screen Images: Snapshot

The cc:Mail Snapshot program lets you show the message recipient the contents of a specific screen from your computer. Once loaded, Snapshot can be used within any program to capture the image of that screen and save it to a file. Once the image file has been created, you can attach the image as an item in a message. You can also use Snapshot to view the image just captured on your screen.

Capturing Screens

These Quick Steps show you how to capture any screen and save it to a file for cc:Mail.

Q Capturing a screen image with Snapshot

1. Change your directory to the cc:Mail subdirectory.

   The DOS prompt changes to something like M:\CCMAIL.

2. Type **SNAPSHOT** and press Enter.

   The Snapshot program is loaded, and Snapshot displays a message on the screen. The DOS prompt appears.

3. Load and begin using a DOS program. When you have a screen to capture, press Alt-1.

   A small screen appears with Take and store snapshot highlighted.

4. Press Enter.

   If the screen contains only text, a prompt appears asking you to type the filename. If the screen is graphic, Snapshot automatically assigns and displays a filename in the current directory.

5. Use Backspace to delete the drive letter if necessary. Type the filename and press Enter.

   A small window containing the filename appears in the upper right corner of the screen.

6. Press Esc or wait three seconds for the window to disappear.

   You can continue using your program after the window is gone. □

147

Snapshot distinguishes between text and graphics screens. As noted, if you are capturing a text screen, you are prompted to provide a filename. If you attach this file to a message, the text screen becomes a text message item and may be edited like any other text message item. If Snapshot detects a graphics screen, the image can be modified only with the Graphic Editor.

The Snapshot program captures one screen at a time in a special cc:Mail format. The saved screen is in a DOS file and, as such, may be copied and deleted like any other DOS file. To attach this file to a message, however, you must select attach Snapshots on the Attach menu. Otherwise, cc:Mail will not recognize and display the image on the recipient's screen. See Chapter 6 for more detail on attaching Snapshots.

The menu selection shown in Figure 7.7 allows you to capture the current text screen or view a previously captured screen. This menu appears only if you are in text mode. If you type a filename that already exists, Snapshot warns you and asks if you want to replace the file. If you type Y for yes, the current screen image replaces whatever was in the original file.

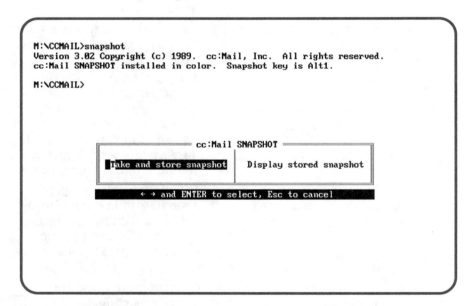

Figure 7.7   The Snapshot menu after pressing Alt-1.

When capturing graphic images, you cannot name the screen capture file. When you press Alt-1, Snapshot automatically names the file using SNAP as the first four letters, the screen type as the next three letters (VGA, EGA, CGA, or HGC), and a number for the extension. This extension number is automatically incremented for each new image in that directory. For example, three images captured on a VGA screen would be named SNAPVGA.001, SNAPVGA.002, and SNAPVGA.003. These files would be saved in the current directory.

If you want to name the screen capture files from DOS yourself, you should use a consistent file naming method and location to save the files. After Snapshot has captured a graphic screen, use the DOS COPY command to copy the file to the designated directory and rename the file at the same time.

For example, assume that you captured a spreadsheet screen in graphics mode while in Quattro Pro. Snapshot saved the screen as SNAPVGA.001. Once you exit Quattro Pro, you'll want to copy the file in a directory you've created to hold your cc:Mail project files. The DOS command and filename would look like this:

```
C:\QPRO>COPY SNAPVGA.001 D:\MAIL\QPROSAMP.SNP
```

The file now exists in both the QPRO directory as SNAPVGA.001 and in the MAIL directory as QPROSAMP.SNP. Once you know that the file is in your working directory (MAIL), you may want to delete the original copy.

149

Viewing Images

You can use Alt-1 to view a previously captured screen from within a program currently displaying text. Remember that Snapshot provides this menu only with a text screen. If the screen is a graphics screen, Snapshot just captures this image and saves it to disk.

After selecting Display stored snapshot from the Snapshot menu, type the complete filename you want to view. Pressing F1 displays the current directory, as shown in Figure 7.8. Notice that you cannot change drives or directories from this screen but can only type a filename shown on this directory list.

Snapshot provides a window reminding you that, once the image is displayed, you can press any key to finish viewing the screen. To remove the window, you can press Esc or just wait three seconds for the window to clear automatically. The image then appears on the screen. After pressing any key, you are returned to the original program screen.

```
                      cc:Mail SNAPSHOT
 Display snapshot stored in file: M:\CCMAIL\                        ◄

 The files with the specified Drive:\Path\Filename.Ext are:
 ADMIN.BAK        MAIL.EXE         MAIL.PIF         MESSENGR.EXE    NOTIFY.COM
 SNAPSHOT.COM     DAN.BAT          ERIK.BAT         MARY.BAT        BACK.EXE
 SNAPVGA.001      LINDA.BAT        KATHY.BAK        STEVE.BAT       TEST
 SNAPVGA.002      SNAPVGA.003      TEST2            NERIK.BAT       NTEST.BAT
 ADMIN.BAT        FAX.~BA          CHECK.BAK        CHECK.BAT       CCM1002.PCX
 SAMSAPPL.TXT     KATHY.BAT        FAX.BAT




     Type the filename and press ENTER, F1 for directory, Esc to cancel
```

Figure 7.8   A sample directory list displayed before viewing a stored Snapshot.

Memory limitations or the original program may keep Snapshot from capturing a graphics screen. If Snapshot cannot capture the screen, pressing Alt-1 just produces a tone. Nothing else happens.

Caution: Once loaded, Snapshot occupies about 27K of memory. If another program will not run after you load Snapshot, you may need to remove Snapshot from memory. If Snapshot was the last program loaded, you can type **SNAPSHOT REMOVE** to free up that memory.

For Windows Users

cc:Mail for Windows includes a notify feature when the program is running. Chapter 5 contains information about changing the Notify Options. Likewise, the ability to capture screens to the Clipboard and to make changes with Paintbrush replace the DOS Snapshot and Graphic Editor. For more information about Clipboard and Paintbrush, refer to your Windows manual.

What You Have Learned

▶ The Notify program automatically checks your cc:Mail Inbox for new messages at regular intervals from 1 to 60 minutes.

▶ The Messenger program also checks for messages and allows you to read and prepare simple messages from within other DOS programs.

▶ The Graphic Editor, part of the Mail program, provides a limited way to create or modify single-screen graphic images.

▶ You must load Snapshot before you can capture screens from other programs. Snapshot remains in memory, waiting for you to initiate an action with the Alt-1 hotkey combination.

151

Using cc:Mail Remote

In This Chapter

► *Installing cc:Mail Remote on a hard drive or floppy disk*
► *Running cc:Mail Remote*
► *Managing your local mailing directory*
► *Sending and receiving messages*
► *Modem troubleshooting*

The cc:Mail Remote program provides access to e-mail messages from outside the network. With cc:Mail Remote and a modem, anyone can send messages to any post office. If the remote caller has a mailbox in the post office, messages are also returned.

There are three kinds of remote callers: local/remote, remote, and outside remote. A local/remote caller has a local mailbox but can call from outside the office to access messages. A remote caller has a mailbox in the post office but can only send and receive mail using cc:Mail Remote. An outside remote user can only send messages to a post office. Messages cannot be returned since they do not have an address in the post office.

cc:Mail Remote provides mailbox access for local users when they are away from the office. When instructed, cc:Mail Remote dials the post office, sends any messages created on the remote computer to mailboxes in the post office, and picks up mail left in the local user's Inbox. Mail sent to the remote location remains in the local Inbox to be handled after the user's return to the office.

For example, suppose you will be out of the office for a week. You decide to take a portable computer with a modem and cc:Mail Remote installed. To receive and respond to messages sent to your mailbox, you need to follow a few more steps than when ordinarily sending and receiving cc:Mail messages:

1. Connect the modem to a phone line and select a menu choice to call your post office. (If you are not sure what a modem is or are taking the computer out for the first time, read the "Modem Troubleshooting" section later in this chapter.)

2. Once the phone call has been made, cc:Mail Remote sends any messages you have created (at this point, none) and then retreives any unread messages from your local Inbox.

3. Once the exchange is completed, cc:Mail Remote hangs up the phone.

4. cc:Mail Remote allows you to examine each message using the same menu choices as Mail (the main cc:Mail program), just as though you were sitting back in your office. You may reply, forward, or temporarily file messages on the local computer.

5. If you respond to messages, you may want to call the post office again. The message exchange will now include the message replies you just made.

6. When you return to the office a week later, you can permanently save or delete the messages in your Inbox.

154

Remote mailbox addresses represent individuals who only use cc:Mail Remote to send and receive messages through the post office. Like local users, remote users have an address in the mailing directory and can send messages to other remote users. Unlike local users, they receive their messages only when they call the post office, and the messages are then deleted from the post office. (Their messages can be stored on the remote computer, however.)

Even without a personal mailbox in a post office directory, remote users can send messages to a post office. This one-way transaction requires the post office name and phone number and at least one mailbox address in the post office mailing directory. To send a message, add the post office name and phone number in the mailing directory as a post office. Then, when you add the name of someone at that post office to your mailing directory, you can send messages to that person. But, because you have no local address in the post office, he or she cannot reply to your messages through cc:Mail. Instead, that person might respond by means of your local fax number, the regular mail, or the phone (assuming you provided your fax number, mail address, or phone number).

> **Tip:** You can send a message addressed to Administrator in any post office if you do not have a specific name in that post office.

Note that many of the features in cc:Mail Remote are the same as those found in Mail or Admin. Although this chapter covers the features unique to cc:Mail Remote, you'll be provided with references to other chapters in this book that cover similar procedures.

Getting Started

155

As a cc:Mail Remote user, you are the system administrator as well as the user. You must copy the files to a suitable disk, set up your user profile, make the proper phone connections, and maintain the mailing directory. If you are using a laptop computer, you may want to set up and test the system in the office. If you are installing cc:Mail Remote on a desktop system, make sure you have someone you can call for help. Try to install and test the software well in advance of the first time you need to use it.

Installation

The cc:Mail Remote software does not use a special installation program. You copy the files to a convenient subdirectory on your hard disk or to a floppy disk. The first time you run the program, you answer several questions relating to your modem, main post office, and text editor defaults.

To start cc:Mail Remote the first time, make sure that you are in the directory containing the program or that the program disk is in the drive and type REMOTE

The first four questions require a typed response. The remaining questions provide a menu choice. In most cases, you can press Enter to accept the highlighted choice. You can also change these answers later with the Change profile menu choice under Manage mailbox in the Main menu.

▶ Type your name as it appears in your home post office mailing directory, typically, your last name, a comma, and your first name. If this does not match, you'll never be able to make the post office connection.

▶ Type your password. If you have a local mailbox, use the same password. If you are a remote-only user and the password does not match the password in the post office mailing directory, you may have to work with the system administrator to make the connection. Once you make the connection, you can change the password in cc:Mail Remote, and it is automatically changed in your post office address. (See Chapter 1 for hints about creating and using passwords.)

▶ Type your home post office name. This, too, must match exactly in order to make the post office connection.

▶ Type your home post office phone number. Include a 1 and the area code if you are dialing long distance. If you are using a PBX system, you may also need a 9 and two commas before the phone number. (Each comma tells the modem to pause three seconds. Some PBX systems need a few seconds to connect to the outside line.) Do not leave spaces in the phone number.

▶ Select the pen color for your text messages. Pressing Enter on a color provides the default of white letters on a blue background.

▶ Select the right and left margins by moving the pointers and then pressing F5 and F6. Pressing Enter sets the margins at 10 and 70.

▶ For the modem type, press Enter to select the Hayes compatible choice unless your system administrator suggests otherwise.

▶ For the telephone type, press Enter to select Touch-tone unless you know you have the older rotary phone lines.

▶ The data rate is likely to be 2400 baud. This speed is the most common. Again, your system administrator may suggest another choice.

▶ You must know the serial (COM*n*:) port for your modem. If you get a Modem not responding message when you select Send/receive messages, change this port to another setting and try again.

▶ The printer port is likely to be LPT1. Change this only if you know the printer is on another port.

▶ For the printer type, select the type of printer you have attached to your computer. If you are not sure what type it is, select Text only.

Once you complete these questions, the Main menu appears as shown in Figure 8.1. If you are familiar with Mail, you can see that the top of the screen is slightly different from the Mail Main menu and that there is one additional menu choice, Send/receive messages.

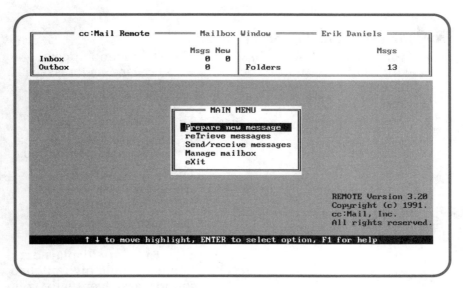

Figure 8.1   The cc:Mail Remote Main menu.

At the top left of the screen, the Inbox count includes the total number of messages and unread messages. These are messages you have picked up from other post offices when you called. The messages remain in the Inbox until you move them to a folder or delete them.

The Outbox count shows the total number of messages you have prepared to be sent. This includes all messages to all post offices. Once you have successfully sent all these messages, this value returns to 0. The top right part of the screen shows the number of messages in folders on your disk. The higher the value, the more disk space is used to keep the messages.

Testing the Connection

Before you begin preparing messages to send, you should test your connection with your home post office. Testing the connection now may prevent a lot of frustration later. The information you just entered must be correct for the connection to work. Use the following Quick Steps to call your home post office. Any unread mail in your Inbox will be transmitted to your computer as part of this call.

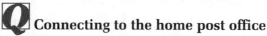 **Connecting to the home post office**

1. From the directory or disk with cc:Mail Remote, type **REMOTE** and your password. Press Enter.

    The Main menu appears with `Prepare new message` highlighted.

2. Select `Send/receive messages`.

    The Send/Receive menu appears with `call Post office/person` highlighted.

3. Press Enter.

    The mailing directory appears with your home post office highlighted.

4. Press Enter.

    The messages `Resetting modem...` and `Placing a call to...` are displayed. You hear some high-pitched sounds, and eventually you see the message `Hanging up telephone`.

5. Press Esc.

    The Main menu appears. □

If you had any messages in the post office, they would be sent and your Inbox count would show the number of messages received. Just before you pressed Esc to return to the Main menu, you should have seen a screen similar to the one in Figure 8.2. If you did not, then one of several settings or connections has not been made properly.

Review the "Modem Troubleshooting" section later in this chapter for suggestions or contact your system administrator for assistance.

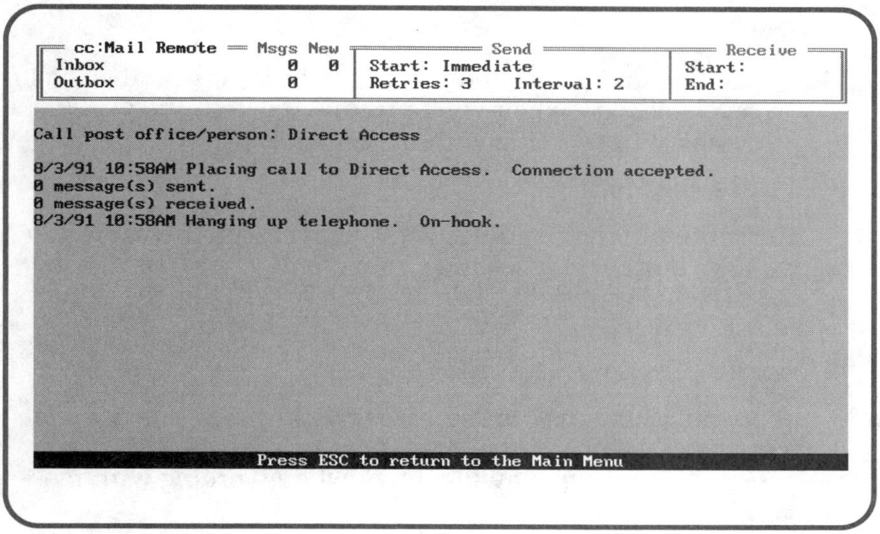

```
┌─ cc:Mail Remote ══ Msgs New ┬═════════ Send ═══════════┬═══════ Receive ═══┐
│ Inbox                 0   0 │ Start: Immediate         │ Start:            │
│ Outbox                0     │ Retries: 3   Interval: 2 │ End:              │
└─────────────────────────────┴──────────────────────────┴───────────────────┘

Call post office/person: Direct Access

8/3/91 10:58AM Placing call to Direct Access.  Connection accepted.
0 message(s) sent.
0 message(s) received.
8/3/91 10:58AM Hanging up telephone.  On-hook.




                        Press ESC to return to the Main Menu
```

Figure 8.2   *Making the connection with the home post office.*

159

The cc:Mail Remote Command Line

The command line to run cc:Mail Remote can contain a number of parameters, including the password, modem settings, and settings for housekeeping tasks. Listed below are a few of the parameters and how they might be used.

REMOTE *password*

Types your password when you start cc:Mail Remote. Instead of the password prompt, the Main menu appears immediately.

REMOTE A:

Tells the program that you are using only one drive to store all messages and folders. Used only with single floppy drive systems.

REMOTE *password* **COMM/CALL**

Calls your home post office and exchanges messages automatically. Useful in batch files.

REMOTE DIAGNOSTICS

Echos modem control and response characters on the screen. This is necessary when you're trying to determine where problems are occurring with the modem.

REMOTE KEYS/*xxx*

Starts the program with the keys represented by *xxx*. If you wanted to prepare a message immediately, you could use **KEYS/PA** to jump right to the mailing list. This is the same as selecting Prepare new message from the Main menu.

REMOTE *password* **RECLAIM**

Reorganizes the disk to increase access speed. You are returned to DOS after using this parameter. Use this if you notice the program slowing down when working with message files.

REMOTE MONO

Sets cc:Mail Remote to black and white. Some systems may appear to the program as color but have only a monochrome screen. MONO may make the screen more readable.

With the exception of RECLAIM, these parameters may be combined on the command line. For example, if you are using a laptop with just one floppy drive, you can type the following command to jump right to the mail directory to select an address:

REMOTE *password* **A: MONO KEYS/PA**

Likewise, you can use the convenient command **REMOTE COMM/CALL** to check your home post office for messages.

Managing Your Mail Directory

Before you can send messages to addresses in your home post office or other post offices, you must add those names to your mailing list.

With the network-based version of cc:Mail, the system administrator performs this task. In cc:Mail Remote, you can maintain your local mailing list in two ways: by keeping a small list of mailboxes, or by adding names one at a time when you first start the program. If your Gateway program has Directory Exchange, you can generate a message requesting an update to your local directory.

Manual Updates

As noted earlier, in order to send a message to anyone with cc:Mail Remote, you must first enter the user's post office name and post office phone number in your mailing directory. You can then send a message by selecting this mailbox name and creating the message. Since this user's location is stored in the directory, cc:Mail Remote knows where to send the message.

These Quick Steps show you how to add a new post office and then a name at that post office. You can't prepare a message to anyone until his or her name appears in the mailing directory.

161

Q Adding an entry to the mailing list in cc:Mail Remote

1. From the Main menu, select `Manage mailbox`.	The Manage menu appears with `manage Mail directory` highlighted.
2. Press Enter.	The Mailing Directory appears.
3. Type the exact post office name.	The location prompt asks if this is `Remote` or `Post office`. The default is `R`.
4. Press P for post office.	The cc:Mail address prompt appears.
5. Type the exact phone number of the post office, including 1 and the area code for long distance. Do not use spaces in the number.	The `Enter comments:` prompt appears.
6. Type any comments to help you identify the post office.	The `Add new name...` prompt appears.
7. Type the name of the person exactly as it appears in that post office.	The location prompt asks if this is `Remote` or `Post office`. The default is `R`.

8. Press Enter or R for Remote.	The Enter cc:Mail address prompt appears.
9. Type the exact name of the post office. (You can't point to the name.)	The Enter comments: prompt appears.
10. Enter any comments.	The Add new name... prompt appears.
11. Continue to add addresses if necessary. When finished, press Esc to return to the Main menu.	The Main menu reappears. □

If you incorrectly enter some of the information, any number of problems might arise. For example, if you forget the post office in the cc:Mail address, you'll get an error message when you try to send a message to that person. If the post office number is wrong or has a space in it, the modem may attempt to dial but will never reach the intended post office.

> **Tip:** If you have a message that cannot be sent, select reTrieve messages from the Main menu and then retrieve from inBox/outbox. The message can then be handled like any message in a folder.

To make changes in an address, select Manage mailbox and then manage Mail directory. To change a remote address or post office, move the highlight to the entry to be corrected and press Enter. The Directory menu appears as shown in Figure 8.3. From this menu, you can change the name, address, or comments.

Automatic Updates

If your home post office has Automatic Directory Exchange, you can have your mailing list updated automatically. You instruct cc:Mail Remote to send a special message the next time you call your post office. When the post office receives this special message, it automatically returns any directory updates made since the date you specified in this message.

To have your directory automatically updated, use the following Quick Steps. You need not make the call to your home post office immediately as part of this process. You can stop after Step 3 and wait until the next time you want to send other messages. The directory update exchange will still occur. Then you can continue with these Quick Steps.

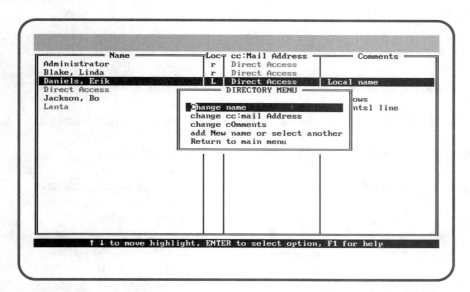

Figure 8.3 *The Directory menu for changing mailing directory entries.*

163

Q Initiating an automatic directory update in cc:Mail Remote

1. From the Manage menu, select manage directory Updates.

   An After date and time prompt appears with the current date and time.

2. Change the date to the last time you updated the directory. If you don't know this date, enter a date that predates your post office.

   A message flashes briefly indicating that a directory update message is being created. The Manage menu appears.

3. Select Return to main menu.

   The Outbox count is increased by one on the Main menu screen.

4. Select Send/receive messages.

   The Send/Receive menu appears with Send all messages highlighted.

5. Press Enter.   cc:Mail Remote places a call to your home post office, sends the message, and receives any directory changes since the date you specified.

6. Press Esc to return to the Main menu.   The `Read inbox messages` selection on the Main menu is highlighted.

7. Press Enter.   The Inbox message list is displayed.

8. Select the message with the Subject Automatic directory update. (This may be the only message in the list.)   The Update menu appears with `Update directory` highlighted.

9. Press Enter.   A prompt asks if you are sure you want to update your directory.

164

10. Press Y.   An update status message is displayed showing the number of updates.

11. Press Enter.   The Update menu returns.

12. To remove the message from the Inbox, either delete it or move it to a folder.   The Main menu reappears.

                       □

Any time you want to update your mailbox, you must request the changes from the system administrator by sending a special message with cc:Mail Remote. Several factors may prevent you from receiving the updates you expected:

▶ If your system administrator has not set Remote user propagation to Yes, you'll not get the changes.

▶ If you forget to change the date with the `Update directory` selection, you'll get the changes that occurred only since you created the message.

▶ If the system administrator did not have or did not activate Automatic Directory Exchange until after the original directory was created, you won't see the entire directory.

▶ If you don't have full access to the post office, you won't receive the directory updates.

▶ If the updates are older than the current entries, you will be
warned that the update is not in sequence. If you proceed,
you might lose new addresses to old changes.

> **Tip:** If you are concerned about the update sequence,
> copy the file MBOXDATA to another name such as
> MBOXDATA.OLD before using cc:Mail Remote to update your
> directory.

> **Tip:** If your system administrator activates the Directory
> Exchange after entering a lot of names, have him or her
> make minor changes in each of the Comments column. The
> name will be recorded as changed, and you will get a copy of the
> entire mailing directory.

165

Once you have received the messages, remember to use the
Update directory choice on the Update menu, which is shown in
Figure 8.4. cc:Mail Remote uses the information in the directory
update message to update your local directory. You can view this
message if you like, but making changes to the text is likely to cause
problems to the update. This message may then be treated like any
other message and moved to a folder or deleted.

If your system administrator has enabled the bulletin board
exchange, you will also receive updated bulletin board messages.
They will appear in your Inbox with the name of the bulletin board
as the title.

> **Caution:** If your post office has a number of active
> bulletin boards, you may not want this feature enabled.
> You could end up with a lot of bulletin board messages and a
> high phone bill as a result.

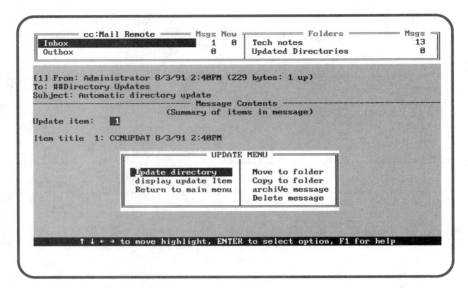

Figure 8.4 The Update menu accessed from the Manage menu.

Sending Messages

To send and receive messages with cc:Mail Remote, you have to initiate a phone call with the Send/receive messages selection on the Main menu. Even if you don't have any messages to send, you may want to "touch base" to pick up any messages. cc:Mail Remote provides several ways to accomplish this. Figure 8.5 shows the Send/Receive menu. The upper portion of the screen provides information about the Inbox, Outbox, and Send and Receive settings.

The quickest way to begin calling is to select SEND ALL MESSAGES. cc:Mail Remote then looks in the Outbox for messages to be sent to other post offices. If it finds messages, it groups them by post office and makes calls to each post office. It then sends the messages, picks up any messages waiting for you in the post office, and places the messages in your Inbox.

If there are no messages in the Outbox, you must select CALL POST OFFICE/PERSON. Your mailing directory appears with your home post office highlighted. You can press Enter to call your home office or select another post office to call. Because there are no messages to send, this call is just to check for messages to you in the post office. If messages are waiting, they are transmitted to your Inbox.

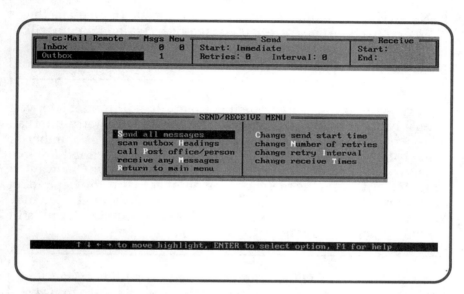

167

Figure 8.5   The Send/Receive menu for checking files and location.

The right side of the menu lists settings that control when your system places the call, how often it dials again if the connection is not made the first time, and how many minutes it waits between tries. The values you select for these settings remain in effect until changed.

If you want to make the calls at a specific time, select Change send start time and then change the setting from Immediate to a specific time. The current system time is then displayed on the screen. Enter a time in 24-hour format or with AM or PM following the hours and minutes. Once you've changed the setting, you must select call Post office/person. cc:Mail Remote then waits until the designated time to make the call. The screen shows the current time as well as the target time.

Once the target time you set is reached, cc:Mail Remote begins calling. This feature is useful if you want to wait for lower phone rates or call an after-hours Gateway connection (for example, one that runs between 5:00 p.m. and 6:00 a.m.). To return to the immediate call, select `Change send start time` and press Enter at the prompt. The status for `Start:` returns to Immediate.

> **Tip:** If you don't change the send time to Immediate, the next time you try to call a post office, cc:Mail Remote will wait until the time you entered previously before making the calls.

Whether or not you are using a send time or Immediate, you probably want to set the number of retries and the retry interval. These are set from their respective menu choices. The number of retries should be set to something larger than 0. If cc:Mail Remote receives a busy signal (which is very likely on an active Gateway), it stops trying to send the message. The number to use will depend on when you call and the message traffic on your post office. You may want to start with four retries at intervals of five minutes. If calls still do not get through, increase these settings.

> **Tip:** Since your computer is tied up while cc:Mail Remote waits to make these calls, you may want to use a send time instead of increasing the tries or the interval. For example, if you're using cc:Mail to transmit orders and receive confirmations, you may want to set the send time for `2:00AM` and just leave the computer on all night.

cc:Mail Remote can also wait for messages instead of initiating the calls for message transfer. Two menu choices on the Send/Receive menu provide this feature. If you select `receive any Messages`, cc:Mail Remote begins waiting for an incoming call. If you set the starting and ending times under `change receive Times`, this waiting mode can be delayed until later. In both cases, the computer cannot be used for anything else because it is busy waiting for the call.

In order to receive messages, you need to plan ahead. The Gateway user or another cc:Mail Remote user must know when you will be in Receive mode as well as your local phone number. Any calls received on that line between the starting and ending times will be answered by the modem. If a person were to call, he or she would hear a high-pitched whine for 30 seconds, and then the modem would hang up. One advantage to using cc:Mail Remote in Receive mode is that the Gateway caller incurs the phone line charge.

Handling Messages

The procedures you use to prepare messages, read Inbox messages, and retrieve messages in cc:Mail Remote are similar to those you use in the Mail program. These topics, and the chapters in which they are covered, are outlined below.

► If electronic mail is new to you, read Chapter 1, "Getting Started with cc:Mail."

► To read messages in your Inbox, read Chapter 2, "Getting Mail."

169

► To prepare messages to send, read Chapter 3, "Sending Mail." Remember that the message is not actually delivered until you select Send/receive messages from the Main menu in cc:Mail Remote.

► To handle messages after you have read them, read Chapter 4, "Dealing with Each Message." The only difference in cc:Mail Remote is that you do not have bulletin boards on your system. You can send messages to bulletin boards in a post office, however. If the system admininstrator has enabled bulletin board transmittal, you'll see bulletin board messages on your system as individual messages.

► The additional tasks for a cc:Mail Remote user are covered in the "Managing Your Mail Directory" section of this chapter. Chapter 5, "Managing Your Mailbox," discusses how to create mailing lists and folders and how to change your profile.

► A cc:Mail Remote user can attach DOS files and graphic images to messages. Chapter 6, "Sending More Than Text," explains this process. The remote user should remember that attaching files increases the size of the message to be transmitted. The message thus takes longer to transmit and costs more as a result.

► To include graphic images and screen images from other programs, read Chapter 7, "Special Features and Programs."

Managing Your Remote Mailbox

You have several additional tasks as a cc:Mail Remote user. As covered earlier in this chapter, you manage your own mailing directory. Before you can send a message to someone, you must have his or her exact name and address. After you prepare the message, you must make the connection by selecting Send/receive messages from the Main menu.

Your messages are also stored differently in cc:Mail Remote. Whereas the network post office has a large master file containing all the messages, your messages are numbered and stored individually on your disk. Although you can delete files at the DOS prompt, cc:Mail Remote will not know that these message files have been deleted. You'll just see the words Message cannot be read in a scan of message headers. A better approach is to delete the files with the reTrieve messages choice from the Main menu. This way the files are deleted from the disk as are any references to them in folders or the Inbox.

Backing up the cc:Mail Remote message files is also up to you. If the messages you receive are important and you want to keep them, you need to develop a system to copy the files to archive disks. With a hard drive system and a limited number of messages, you can use the following commands to copy all the critical files to a floppy disk in drive A:

```
COPY ????DATA A:
COPY MSG* A:
```

If you have a large number of messages to back up, you need to use a program specifically for backing up large or numerous files to floppy disk.

If you use a floppy disk system, the easiest way to create a backup of the files is to copy the original disk or disks, label them, and then put the copied disks away. As with hard disk backup disks, always keep several sets and rotate the set each time you make the backup copies.

170

Modem Troubleshooting

A modem converts the signals created by the computer into a signal that can travel over the phone lines. The modem on the other computer converts that phone line signal back into a signal for the computer. For cc:Mail Remote to work, this connection must be successfully established and maintained.

The modem may either be built into the computer or connected to it as a separate box. If a modem is built-in, you'll see one or two telephone jacks in the back or the side of your computer. If you have an external modem, that modem will have a cable attaching it to the computer and may have a power cord as well.

Both an internal and external modem have telephone jacks, which require special phone plugs called RJ-11 connectors. One jack (socket) may be marked as "Line" and the other "Phone." The phone cord must be plugged into the line jack, but a phone may or may not be plugged into the phone jack. You can use a phone plugged into the phone jack anytime except when the modem is being used. In this case, the modem takes over the phone line, and the phone will be dead.

Either modem uses a serial port in your system. (A port is how the computer communicates with the outside world.) Most systems have from one to four serial ports referred to as COM1:, COM2:, COM3:, and COM4:. Other devices such as a printer and a mouse may also be attached to a serial port. Unless someone made a note on the COM port next to the phone jack, there is no way to know which COM port has the modem without trial and error.

When a modem call is first connected, you typically hear a dial tone, the numbers being dialed, a series of high-pitched tones, and then static. Once the modems on each end of the connection have "locked in," the local modem speaker is turned off. Some very small external modems, called pocket modems, are not large enough to have speakers and may not make these sounds.

Communication problems can occur in any number of ways. Use the following steps if you are unable to connect with your post office using cc:Mail Remote. After trying each step, select Send/receive messages again from the Main menu.

1. If the modem is external, check to make sure the power is on. (Internal modems get their power from inside the computer.)

171

2. Check the phone cord from the modem to the wall. Make sure the cord is in the "line" jack in the back of the modem.

3. Check both the line and the phone jack by unplugging the line from the back of the modem and plugging it into a phone. Listen for a dial tone. If custom-made (instead of purchased), you might have a dead cable.

4. If the modem is external, check the cable connections from the back of the modem to the computer.

5. Change the COM port setting. Change the setting to the next highest number, for example, from COM1: to COM2:. If it is on COM4:, return the setting to COM1:.

6. Change the baud rate to a lower setting. If set at 2400, reset to 1200.

7. Check the phone system dialing procedure. Your phone numbers may need a 9 or 8 before the number. If they do, use that number and two commas. The number may look like 9,,1-317-555-1212.

8. If you reach the post office but get a message that the connection was refused, you may not have proper access to the post office. Ask your system administrator for your password in the mailing directory, then set your local password to the same. After you make the connection the first time, change your local password. It will be changed in the post office as well.

9. Check to make sure you have the right phone number for the post office.

10. If possible, use another communications program to check the modem and phone line.

11. If you make the connection and begin sending or receiving messages and then lose the connection, the phone line may contain lots of static. Make the call again. If the problem continues, contact the phone company.

12. Use the DIAGNOSTICS parameter on the command line to note the signals being sent to the modem as well as over the phone line.

13. If you get disconnected during a phone call, check for Call Waiting on the phone line. The Call Waiting signal tells the modem to disconnect. Many phone systems use *70 to disable Call Waiting for the duration of the call. Check with your local phone company for confirmation.

14. If you intend to use the computer while traveling, be aware that many hotel rooms do not have the proper phone jack to make the connection. You can purchase a special kit to compensate for this problem.

What You Have Learned

▶ cc:Mail Remote allows local and remote users to send and receive messages through a post office.

▶ The program can be installed and run on a hard drive or on a dual or single floppy drive.

▶ The command line can contain several parameters, the most convenient of which is to include your password after the word **REMOTE**.

▶ Because you are also the administrator of your mailing list, you have to add names or request updates from your post office.

▶ Reading, handling, and sending messages in cc:Mail Remote involve essentially the same steps as in the Mail program. Messages are not sent until the phone connection has been made with the post office.

▶ Modems are an essential part of the communications channel. Until the modem and phone connections work properly, messages cannot be sent or received.

173

Using the cc:Mail Fax Products

In This Chapter

- ▶ *Sending fax messages*
- ▶ *Viewing fax items*
- ▶ *Printing faxes*
- ▶ *Reusing fax files*
- ▶ *Installing and administering cc:Fax and FaxView*

The cc:Fax program provides cc:Mail users with the ability to send facsimile, or fax, messages as cc:Mail messages. Any text or graphic item may be attached as part of the message to be faxed. A DOS file item will be listed on the fax message but will not be transmitted.

This means that you can send a fax message without printing the document, walking to the fax machine, dialing the number, and waiting for the fax machine to scan and transmit the document. You can just select the cc:Fax post office, type the recipient's name and fax number, and create a standard cc:Mail message. cc:Mail then routes that message through the Gateway program, and the message is faxed.

You can also receive fax messages through cc:Fax. A computer dedicated to running Gateway (sending and receiving fax files) accepts the fax image file and routes it to the fax administrator. This individual then determines to whom the fax is addressed and routes the fax to that Inbox. The fax can then be printed, or it can be displayed on a graphics screen with the second cc:Mail program, FaxView.

Check with your system administrator to determine if the cc:Mail fax software package has been installed in your post office. You'll need to know the fax post office name, typically FAX, in order to send messages as facsimiles. You'll also need a graphics screen if you want to be able to display fax messages.

Caution: Unlike cc:Mail messages, fax items may be seen by other people. When you send a fax, someone typically distributes the fax pages. On the receiving end, your fax administrator must look at the fax to route the file to the proper cc:Mail user.

176

Sending Fax Messages

To send a message to any fax machine, you need only know the fax machine phone number. That number becomes part of the To: line of the message along with the recipient's name. Your system administrator can also create post office addresses for frequently used fax machines. Everyone in the cc:Mail network can then use a fax address as part of the address in his or her message.

Messages may contain text and graphic images as part of the fax. If a DOS file is attached to the message, the filename will be listed on the fax along with the text item, but the file itself will not be transmitted.

These Quick Steps assume that your post office includes a post office called FAX to transmit fax messages.

 Transmitting a fax

1. From the Main menu, select Prepare new message.

The Address menu appears with Address to person highlighted.

2. Select the fax post office address line by highlighting F AX and pressing Enter.

   The screen displays the To: prompt.

3. Type the name of the person to receive the fax message, the keyword FAX#, and the number of the fax machine. Press Enter.

   The Address Directory reappears with the highlight remaining on the fax post office.

4. Press Esc.

   The Address menu appears with eNd addressing highlighted.

5. Press Enter.

   The prompt moves to the Subject: line.

6. Enter the subject text and press Enter.

   The cursor moves to the Message Contents area.

7. Continue to create the message as you would any cc:Mail message.

□   **177**

Caution: The message just created will be sent according to the Gateway message transmittal schedule. This schedule is determined by the system administrator and may vary from five minutes to once a day. Check with your system administrator about this schedule. You cannot promise a fax recipient a fax message "within 10 minutes" if the transmit schedule is only every hour.

The text message is converted into a graphic image for the fax transmission. All fax messages contain a cover sheet that includes the address information as well as a graphic image on the top half of this sheet. The cc:Fax program includes the special PCX file shown in Figure 9.1. Your system administrator can change this image using any PCX paint program. Figure 9.2 shows a different cover sheet image.

Graphic images created by the Graphic Editor and Snapshot can also be included in a message for a fax machine. These graphic items are automatically translated into the proper format to send as a fax.

You can also send DOS files with the extension PCX as items in your fax message. If cc:Fax is available on your system, cc:Mail offers an additional selection on the Attach menu, `attach Fax item`. Selecting this choice provides a list of PCX files in the current directory. You can use the Arrow keys to move within that directory or type the full path and filename for the file. The filename must have a PCX extension. Once selected, the image is displayed on the screen. If the file is not in the monochrome PCX format, cc:Mail produces a warning message.

178

Figure 9.1   The top of the standard cc:Fax cover sheet.

Figure 9.2   An alternate cover sheet PCX file.

A number of graphic programs create files with the PCX extension. If you create original fax images with a program such as PC Paintbrush IV Plus, keep these points in mind:

► Create the image in black and white only. Color translations are extremely unpredictable.

► The image should be a maximum of six inches across by eight inches down.

▶ Use a minimum of grays in the image. Some fax machines do not have the resolution to produce gray tones well.

▶ Avoid large areas of black.

▶ Remember that several people are likely to see the image before it gets to your recipient.

▶ You may want to send your first few tries to a local machine to view the results of your efforts.

Receiving Fax Messages

A fax message is retained in electronic form when received by the cc:Mail post office. Because the sender (using a paper-based fax machine) can designate only the fax phone number, there is no way to route the fax directly to you electronically. As a result, all fax images are sent to the fax administrator, who must examine each fax for the name of the recipient and send a message with the fax file attached.

179

Fax files are saved in the post office with a limit of one page per message item and a total of 20 items. If an incoming fax message contains more than 20 pages, those excess pages will be included in a separate message. The administrator typically just forwards the entire message.

How quickly you receive a fax message depends on how often the designated fax administrator reviews the incoming fax files. An active fax port might require constant attention for fax messages to be delivered in a timely manner. In this case, the fax administrator could use the cc:Mail Notify program to find out when faxes are received. Then the faxes could be quickly routed to the intended recipients.

The fax administrator's job of reading and rerouting faxes may be time-consuming. If so, the system administrator can easily reassign this job by using the alias capability to rotate these responsibilities among users on a daily basis.

Viewing with FaxView

Messages with fax items attached contain an x on the message line. You handle that message like any multi-item message. To view the fax image on your screen, simply select that item. Figure 9.3 shows a rerouted fax message just before viewing the fax. If you do not have a graphics screen, your Inbox message lines may include the x for fax, but cc:Mail will not be able to display the fax. You may still be able to print the fax, however, as noted in the next section.

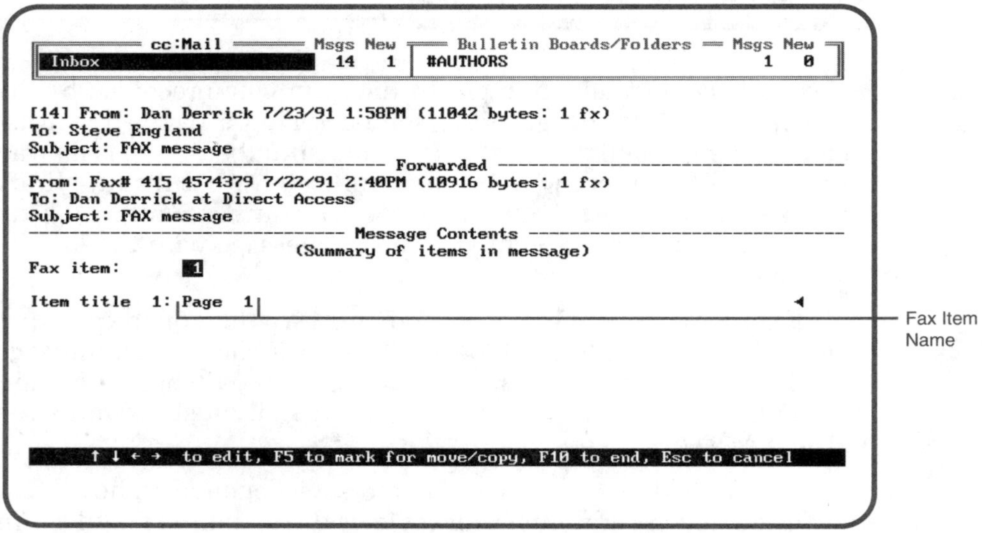

Figure 9.3   A message with a fax attached.

The fax image consists of small dots arranged to form the image. Because fax items are graphic, your ability to read the image is based on the type of screen. The sharper the screen, the more easily readable the fax. Figure 9.4 shows a page of fax image.

The plus (+) and minus (–) keys enlarge and reduce the image. To increase the page size to 1-to-2, press +. To move the image within the screen, use the Arrow and Ctrl keys. Figure 9.5 shows this larger image.

Press + again to enlarge the image to a 1-to-1 size. The text in the fax image shows extreme details, as you can see in Figure 9.6. You must use the Arrow keys to read across and down the screen.

The small square at the bottom of the screen shows the relative position of the screen within the document.

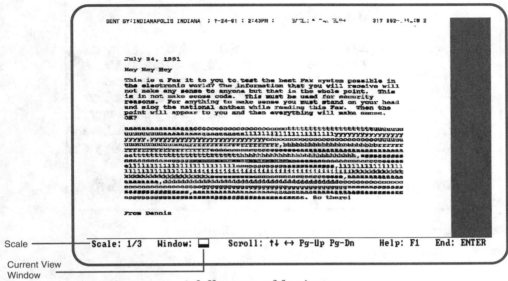

Scale

Current View
Window

181

Figure 9.4   A full screen of fax image.

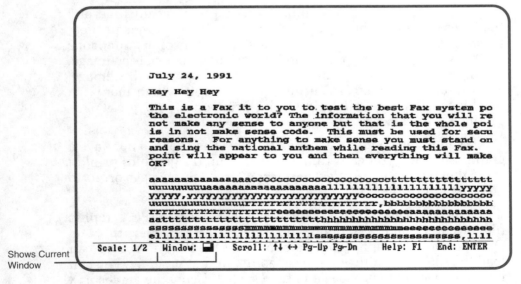

Shows Current
Window

Figure 9.5   A 1-to-2 enlargement of the fax image.

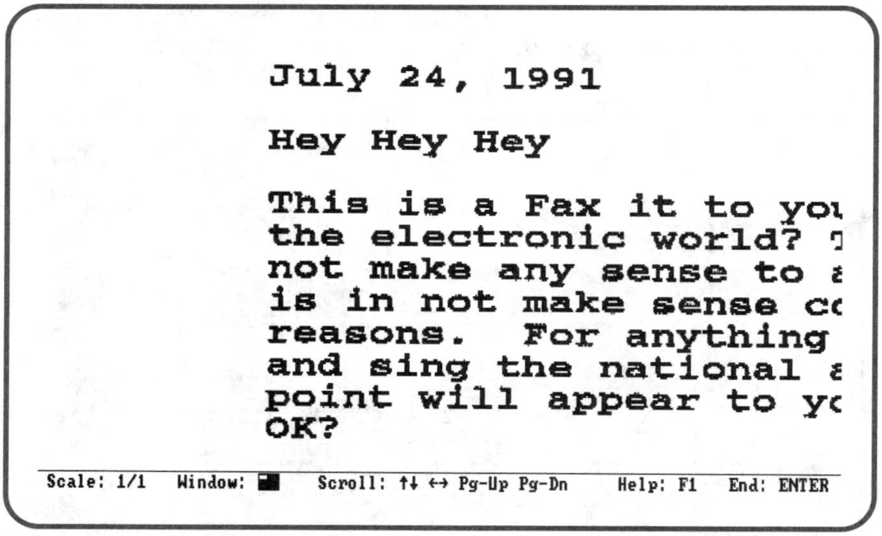

```
            July 24, 1991

            Hey Hey Hey

            This is a Fax it to you
            the electronic world? 1
            not make any sense to a
            is in not make sense co
            reasons.  For anything
            and sing the national a
            point will appear to yo
            OK?
```

| Scale: 1/1 | Window: ■ | Scroll: ↑↓ ↔ Pg-Up Pg-Dn | Help: F1 | End: ENTER |

182

Figure 9.6   The fax image magnified three times.

Printing, Saving, and Changing Faxes

To print the fax image on a graphics printer, press P at any time, and the image is sent to the default printer. The whole page is printed, regardless of the current view. The quality of the fax image depends on the type of graphics printer and the original fax machine image. A nine-pin dot matrix printer may produce a low-quality image. Most laser printers create an image that is better than many fax machines. If the default printer can print only text, pressing P produces only a beep.

Even if you cannot view a fax item because you do not have a graphics screen, you can still print that item to a graphics printer. From the Action menu, select print faX item. The fax page prints to your default printer.

The fax image can also be saved as a DOS file in the PCX graphic file format. From the Action menu, select cOpy fax item to file. Once saved, any graphics program that uses the PCX file format can load the file. Depending on the capability of that program, you can make changes to that image and then save it. Using the attach faX item selection from the Attach menu, you could then resend the file as a fax item. Figure 9.7 shows a fax file with modifications made using Publisher's Paintbrush 2.0.

> ![pencil icon] **Tip:** Because fax messages are stored with a limit of one page per item, you may want to print all the fax items in the message at one time. From the Action menu, select Print message. Since each page of fax can take over a minute to print, a message with several fax items will prevent you from using your system while the images are being printed.

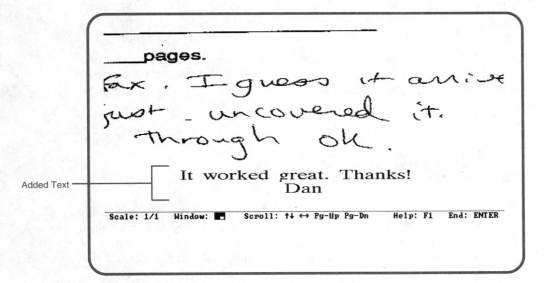

Added Text

Figure 9.7   A modified fax image.

When modifying a PCX fax file, you need to consider several points:

► Keep the file in black and white. Some programs try to convert the image to 4, 16, or 256 colors.

► Don't change the size of the image. Any increase in width or length is cut off when the file is converted for fax transmission.

► A fax PCX image is very large, 1728-by-2348 pixels. Some graphics programs will not be able to read the file.

► Use the text feature to make notes in the margin and then draw a line to the part of the image or text you are commenting on.

Fax versus Text Items

The image on a page is converted to a series of dots when transmitted as a fax. These dots are reconstructed on the receiving end as a graphic image. Any text on the page is just part of that image. That text cannot be used as part of a message item or exported to an ASCII file.

Some character recognition programs can read fax images from the graphic image with varying degrees of accuracy, in some cases, up to 98 percent. But, in all cases, someone must read the resulting text file for accuracy against a printed copy of the fax image.

These same programs can also extract text from a fax file, but this is a separate step that does not involve the cc:Mail software. Once extracted, the text can be used as a text item in a message.

184 System Administration

One copy of cc:Fax provides fax capabilities for all the cc:Mail users on the network. Any cc:Mail user can create and send fax messages to any fax machine. Users with graphic screens can receive and view fax images. Anyone using a graphics printer can print copies of the fax images.

Installation

cc:Fax requires cc:Gateway, a fax board compatible with Communications Applications Specification (CAS), a dedicated network station for the Gateway program, and a dedicated phone line. Before installing cc:Fax, make sure that both Gateway and the fax board work individually. Once cc:Fax is installed, Gateway uses the fax board to send and receive faxes as well as other Gateway functions.

cc:Fax requires a specific fax board that contains a coprocessor to handle the actual fax file transmission. The Gateway program converts and passes the file to the fax board, which then calls the receiving fax machine and monitors the transmission.

For cc:Fax to work properly, you need to make one entry in the post office address list and one entry in the Gateway call list. The address entry creates a special post office with the cc:Mail address of FAXLINK. When users address a message to that post office name, typically FAX, they are prompted for the individual's name and the complete fax machine number. Without this post office, messages cannot be sent as faxes.

The Gateway call list entry (the fax post office name) instructs Gateway to look for fax messages at the specified interval. If the fax post office is not included in the call list, the fax messages are never sent. You may also want to let your users know how often fax messages are sent.

Optionally, you may want to create a specific address line for the fax administrator. When fax messages arrive in the post office box, they are routed to the fax administrator. If that address in not in the directory, the fax is addressed to you, the system administrator. To assign the task of routing fax messages to another user, use the alias function. If you use this address as a unique user name, it takes a user slot in the address count.

cc:Fax comes with a fax cover sheet logo named MAILLOGO.PCX. (See Figure 9.1.) If you want to create a unique logo for your company, you can use any program to make this change, including PC Paint in Windows. To make sure that you create the proper-sized file, copy this file as a backup copy (LOGO-OLD.PCX) and then use the MAILLOGO.PCX file.

185

Administration

Even after cc:Fax has been installed and is working, it requires constant attention. Incoming fax messages are all sent to the system administrator or fax administrator, who must read the first page of the fax to determine the recipient. Then the FAX message must be forwarded to the intended recipient.

Although you may hope that everyone eventually becomes an e-mail user, many people will continue to rely on faxes for quick delivery of information. With a paper-based fax machine, one person can agree to send a fax while the other waits at the fax machine. With the individual intervention needed to distribute the faxes via cc:Mail, an irritating delay may occur in this information flow. If you want to keep your cc:Mail and cc:Fax users content, you need to develop a system for timely delivery of messages.

For example, you may develop a schedule for a Fax-Administrator-of-the-Day (FAD). By changing the fax administrator's cc:Mail address in the mail list to that of another user, the fax administrator becomes an alias for that user. All fax messages are then sent to that individual. Using a combination of Notify and Mail, that person can respond to incoming messages and quickly reroute the fax. The FAD will be more effective if that person spends the majority of the time near the computer system.

A more extreme approach would be to allow everyone access to the fax administrator's mailbox. In this case, that address would require a separate user status. By announcing the password, anyone could read all the fax messages. Once located, the fax could then be forwarded to the user's mailbox. And, as with the paper-based fax machine, other fax messages could be distributed to users if time and interest permit.

186 *Message Privacy*

Keeping fax messages confidential requires a conscious effort. The rotating responsibilities and open access of fax administration obviously do not create a secure fax message system. As in the paper-based fax system, there should be minimal opportunity for others to see faxes if these materials are to be kept private and confidential.

The fax administrator should be fully aware of the need for maintaining privacy with faxes. That individual must also be knowledgeable about the cc:Mail system. For example, if the fax administrator accidentally sends a fax to a bulletin board or mailing list, this lowers the credibility of the system. To help establish a sense of security for everyone in the post office, you might consider providing a written assurance to all users that fax messages are handled in a confidential manner. Of course, you must also ensure that FADs actually follow your guidelines for maintaining confidentiality.

For Windows Users

Messages created with the Windows version of cc:Mail can also be faxed. The restrictions are the same as for the DOS version. Just select the cc:Fax post office and complete the To: line with the fax number, as shown in Figure 9.8. The Gateway program then sends the fax message based on the call table schedule established by the system administrator.

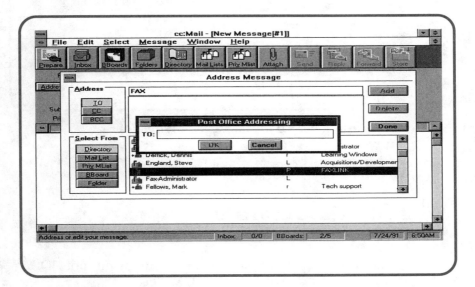

187

Figure 9.8   Sending a fax message in Windows.

Fax messages can also be viewed from within Windows. Figure 9.9 shows part of a half-page fax displayed as a graphic image in Windows. You can resize FAX images from 1-to-1 to 4-to-1 ratios with the + and – keys or by pressing 1, 2, 3, or 4 for the appropriate ratio.

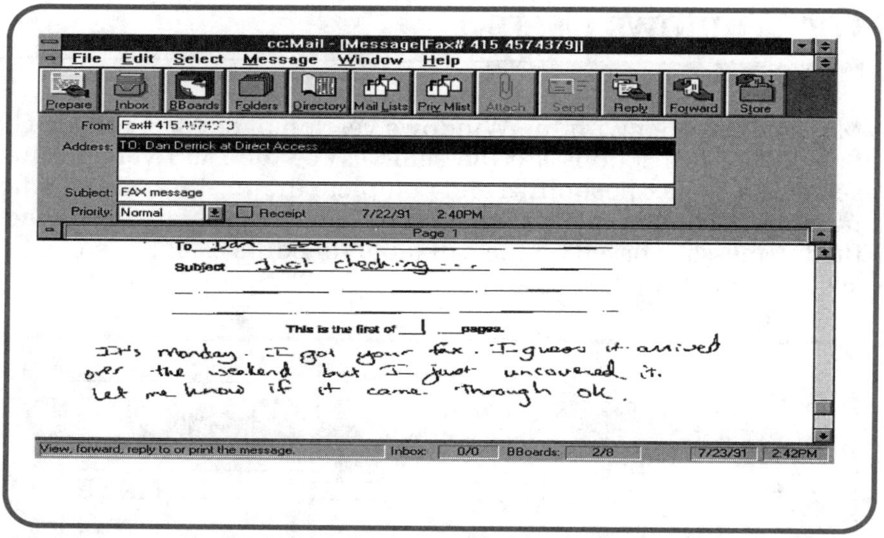

Figure 9.9   Viewing a fax message in Windows.

What You Have Learned

▶ Fax messages transmit text and graphic items but not DOS files. Graphic items can include PCX files.

▶ You can send a message to any fax machine number.

▶ Messages are transmitted automatically based on the schedule established by the system administrator.

▶ Incoming fax messages are routed through the fax administrator. The sender can designate only the fax machine, not the receiver.

▶ Fax items can be saved, changed, and re-sent as monochrome PCX graphic files.

▶ The level of privacy for fax messages depends on your company's approach to fax messages.

Chapter 10

An Administrator's Guide to Managing cc:Mail

189

In This Chapter

- ▶ *Managing mailing directories*
- ▶ *Building public mailing lists*
- ▶ *Creating bulletin boards*
- ▶ *Changing the post office profile*
- ▶ *Providing training and support*

As the cc:Mail system administrator, you manage the network equivalent of a post office. Although you do not need to sort the mail and place it in individual mailboxes, you do need to perform a number of tasks to keep this hub of the e-mail system working smoothly. Once cc:Mail is installed, you must create and maintain the post office mailing directory, the public mailing lists, and the public bulletin boards. And, as with any network-related responsibilities, you should make sure that all the post office database files are backed up on a regular basis.

If your post office exchanges messages with other cc:Mail post offices or other e-mail services, you'll be responsible for managing the cc:Mail Gateway program. If you have the cc:Mail fax products, you will be responsible for rerouting all the incoming fax items. And, regardless of how many or how few mailboxes you have in your post office, you will be the focal point for user training and support.

This chapter covers the main tasks accomplished with the Admin program. Chapter 11 covers the other programs supplied with the Platform Pack and other cc:Mail administration-level programs.

The opening screen in the Admin program contains post office statistics and the Main menu, as shown in Figure 10.1. The upper part of the screen provides a profile of the post office. The left side of the Main menu contains selections for maintenance tasks on the mailing directory. The right side relates to post office settings.

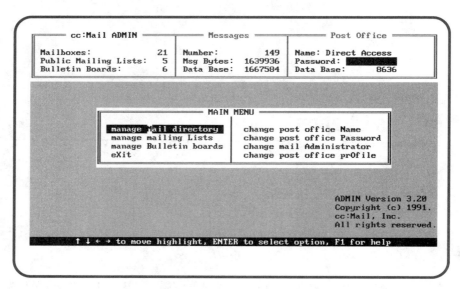

Figure 10.1   The opening screen of the Admin program.

Managing Mailing Directories

The mailing list within cc:Mail is limited to the names you, the administrator, create. Local users with access to the post office can send messages only to other addresses on the mailing list. The number of mailboxes is limited by the software. A copy of the Platform Pack provides one mailbox. Additional mailboxes can be added by purchasing one or more 8 User or 25 User Packs, which, when run, increase the maximum number of mailboxes in the post office by the package number.

Naming Conventions and Aliases

If you are adding names for the first time, you need to decide what format you want to use for the names. This might be last name followed by first name, first name followed by last name, or first initial followed by last name. Whatever method you use, remember that cc:Mail automatically alphabetizes those names.

The number of addresses in the mailing list is unlimited. An address may be a specific mailbox, a post office, a remote user, or an alias. For example, if you purchased one Platform Pack and an 8 User Pack, you could have up to nine mailboxes in the mailing directory. Each individual cc:Mail user might have a mailbox identified by last name and then first name. But, to make indentifying those people easier, each one might also use his or her first name as an alias address. This address would then relate back to the real mailbox address. For example, Mary Smith would be listed as `Smith, Mary`, for her mailbox. Her alias would be `Mary`, which points back to `Smith, Mary`, for the mailbox name. Users could address the message to `Smith, Mary`, or just to `Mary`.

The following Quick Steps show you how to add a name to the mailing directory and how to create an alias for that name. These steps require access to the directory with the cc:Mail administration programs, the name of the post office, and the post office password.

> **Caution:** When starting ADMIN, you must specify the path (location) of the post office. Specifying a different path causes a new post office database to be created.

Q **Adding a name and alias to the mailing list**

1. Move to the drive and sub-directory with the cc:Mail Admin program. It might be `M:\CCADMIN`.	The DOS prompt changes to show that drive and direc-tory.

191

2. Type **ADMIN**.

The prompt `Post office name:` appears.

3. Type the name of your post office.

The `Password:` prompt appears.

4. Type the post office password.

The Main menu appears with `manage Mail directory` highlighted.

5. Press Enter.

The current mailing list appears.

6. Type the new mailbox name using the naming convention you've chosen. If you have names in the mailing list, the highlight may jump around in an effort to find the name as you type.

The location prompt asks if this is `Local`, `Remote`, or `Post office`. The default is `L`.

192

7. Select `Local`.

The Comments line appears. If you have exceeded your allowable number of mailboxes, an error message appears.

8. Enter a description of this address. It may be a job title or department.

The `Add new name:` prompt appears.

9. Type the alias for the name just entered, typically the first name.

The location prompt asks if this is `Local`, `Remote`, or `Post office`. The default is `L`.

10. Press R for `Remote` and then press Enter.

The `Enter comments:` prompt appears.

11. Enter comments for this alias name.

The `Enter cc:Mail address:` prompt appears.

12. Type the original mailbox name.

The location column changes from r (remote) to a (alias) and the `Add new name:` prompt reappears.

13. To return to the Main menu, press Esc.

The Main menu reappears.

☐

Remote and Shared Mailboxes

All cc:Mail users depend on the system administrator to manage the mailing directory. You are the only one who can add, change, and delete mailbox and alias addresses. If users need to send messages to users in other post offices, you have to add that post office and user name in your local mailing directory. But, because this involves long distance phone charges, you may also be the person who establishes the policy for post office message exchanges.

You also determine who will have his or her own mailbox and who must share a mailbox. For example, the people in the mail room may not need to have mail directed to a specific person. Their address and mailbox might just be Mailroom. But, because someone may want to send a message to a specific worker in the mail room, each individual's name can be used as an alias with the Mail room mailbox as the address. The disadvantage, of course, is that everyone in the mail room can read all the mail sent to that mailbox address. Adding a comment such as "Mail room Group" to each line of the alias name makes it clearer that that individual name belongs to a group mailbox.

193

Changing a Mailing Address

Once created, an address line can be changed in a number of ways. You can highlight or type the name and press Enter to bring up the Directory menu in Figure 10.2. This menu allows you to change the name, location, password, and comments and to add a new name. The complete address line can also be deleted from this menu.

The name might be changed to reflect a marriage or to assign the mailbox to another person. cc:Mail retains that local (internal) mailbox number. Any pending messages to the old name would be waiting for the new person using the mailbox. For this reason, you should delete the old name first. Otherwise, you would have to change the password, enter cc:Mail as that individual, and delete all the messages and folders. This also removes the old name from any mailing lists.

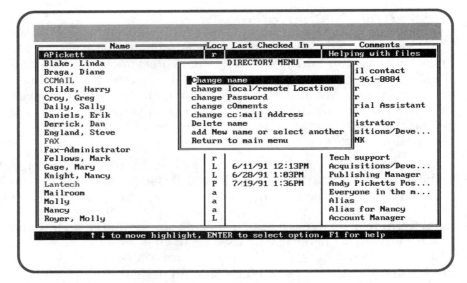

Figure 10.2   The Directory Menu available from the Main menu.

194

Tip: If you want to save an individual's messages and folder but want to release that local slot to another user, change the old name to Remote. The local slot is now available and the old address messages and folders are still intact.

Password and Security Policies

The ability of the administrator to change the password raises the issue of confidentiality. The administrator does not need to know the original mailbox password to make this change. Once a password is changed, the administrator can sign on as that user and read all messages attached to that mailbox. The user must then be informed of the new password in order to use his or her mailbox again.

A specific, written policy statement concerning the privacy of the messages in the cc:Mail system should be prepared and distributed to all users. Because the administrator can read each mailbox only after changing the user's password, the policy should explain why this would occur and what notice, if any, would be provided.

If users are to assume that any messages sent through the company-owned cc:Mail system are the property of the company, that should also be stated. Likewise, this policy document should indicate if messages will be permanently backed up. Before using the cc:Mail system, users should read and acknowledge this policy document.

Building Public Mailing Lists

One extremely powerful feature of e-mail is the ability to send the same message to many people at once. The mailing lists you create in the mailing directory provide that "one shot" address that allows users to send messages to dozens of addresses. You, the administrator, create these public lists that everyone can use.

These lists are likely to overlap in many ways. For example, you may create lists for each mailbox address within each department. You may also create a list for senior management. The senior manager in each department would appear in both these mailing lists.

195

When determining the structure of the public lists in the mailing directory, you should consider several key points:

▶ Everyone should have access to all the public mailing lists.

▶ Be careful how many times a person's name is duplicated on multiple mailing lists. Although the same message sent through two lists to the same person won't be duplicated, more appearances on more lists will mean more mail.

▶ Provide enough information in the Comments column so that the common thread between the addresses is clear.

▶ Occasionally ask users for suggested mailing lists.

▶ Names deleted or changed in the directory are automatically updated in the mailing lists.

▶ You are limited to 200 lists and 200 names per list.

▶ Each mailing list name is limited to 29 characters.

The following Quick Steps show you how to create a mailing list in the mailing directory. The first step assumes you are at the Main menu in the Admin program.

Q **Creating a mailing list in the mailing directory**

1. Select manage mailing Lists.

The highlight appears on the left side of the screen. The prompt for the new name automatically begins with #.

2. Type the new mailing list name and press Enter.

The mailing directory appears with the Add new name: prompt.

3. Select the first name to add to the list and press Enter.

That name appears at the top of the screen and the Add new name: prompt reappears.

4. Continue to add names to build the mailing list.

Each name is added to the list at the top of the screen.

5. Press Esc to finish adding names to this new mailing list.

The Mailing List menu appears.

6. Select Return to main menu.

The Main menu appears. □

Mailing lists and bulletin boards appear together on the screen shown in Figure 10.3, which is used to modify both. In this case, only the left side of the screen is active, as noted by the highlight on that side. To make changes to an existing list, highlight that list name and press Enter. The Mailing List menu appears on the right side of the screen (covering up the unused Bulletin Boards list).

This menu allows you to view, add, and erase names from the mailing list. You can also change and delete the mailing list title. Individual names do not need to be maintained. The name is automatically changed in the mailing list when changed in the mailing directory. If you delete an old user's name, that name is also deleted from the mailing list.

Tip: To make a copy of the mailing list, load Snapshot before beginning Admin. Once the list is displayed with View mailing list, press Alt-1 to create a text file image of the list. You can then convert this file to an ASCII file if you want to print the list.

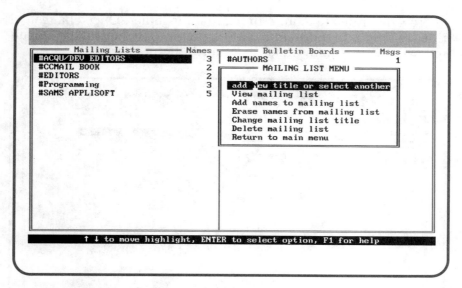

Figure 10.3   The Mailing List menu.

Creating Bulletin Boards

Bulletin boards are used like common folders. Everyone within the post office can place and read messages in bulletin boards, which have different titles to distinguish one "group folder" from another.

You can create up to 200 bulletin boards, each of which can contain 32,767 messages. Messages posted on a board can be handled like any mail messages except that they can be deleted only by you, the administrator, or the original sender.

Once you select manage Bulletin boards from the Main menu of the Admin program, you see the prompt Add a new title: followed by the # character. Because the Bulletin Boards list is alphabetized like the Address and Mailing lists, the # character places those titles at the top of the list. The users' folder names then appear in alphabetical order below the bulletin board names.

If you select an existing bulletin board name by highlighting that name and pressing Enter, the Bulletin Board menu appears, as shown in Figure 10.4. From this menu you can change a bulletin board title or delete a bulletin board all together. Once changed, a title may move to a different location on the alphabetical list, but all messages will remain under that new bulletin board title.

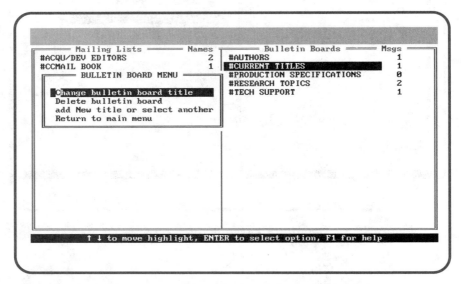

Figure 10.4   The Bulletin Board menu.

If you highlight a bulletin board title and select Delete bulletin board, you'll see the confirmation prompt Are you sure you wish to delete the bulletin board? Pressing Y immediately deletes the board and all the messages it contains. Pressing N returns you to the Bulletin Board menu. Any other key produces an error message.

Caution: Once a bulletin board is deleted, all messages it contains are also deleted. You cannot recover the messages from the current post office files.

Changing Post Office Defaults

Your post office has several default settings that were established when the program was first installed. These include the post office name, the access password, the administrator's name, and the post office and user settings.

Menu choices to make these changes are on the right side of the Main menu of the Admin program. If you make changes to the post office name or password, do so with caution. The post office name is used as the first step to gain access to Admin and is essential for remote access. If the name is changed, all remote users and post offices must use the new name to access the post office.

> **Caution:** Notify all remote users and post offices before changing your post office name. Otherwise, they will be unable to access your post office.

The post office name can have up to 20 characters, including spaces. If you use spaces, however, you will not be able to run Admin from a command line. For example, if the post office is named MCP Sales, the following command line does not work:

```
ADMIN MCP SALES password M:\CCDATA
```

199

The Admin program sees the post office name as MCP and prompts for the correct name. If, on the other hand, the post office name is MCP_Sales or MCP-Sales, the command line will work.

> **Tip:** If you forget the name of your post office, use Mail to view the name at the top of the Mail Main menu. Then use that name to access the post office with Admin.

> **Caution:** Without the post office password, you cannot manage the post office. The only reason for changing the password is to maintain security if the administrator is replaced or if company policy requires such a change periodically. If you forget the password, you'll have to regenerate the entire post office over again, losing all messages and directories.

Error messages are addressed to the administrator's name, as are fax messages if cc:Fax is installed and a mailbox named Fax-Administrator has not been created. Because Admin can be used by anyone with the post office password, the administrator need not be the individual running this program.

The post office profile sets a number of parameters for the post office. Of these five groups of settings, the Default Printer and Default Editor Setting may be changed by the user. The others— Security, Directory Propagation, and Miscellaneous—relate to the way the post office runs. Figure 10.5 shows the profile without Directory Propagation (also called Automatic Directory Exchange) active. Figure 10.6 shows the profile with Directory Propagation active. Directory Propagation is covered in more detail in Chapter 11, "Programs for Administrators."

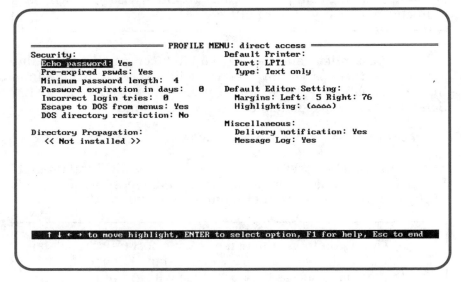

Figure 10.5   The Profile Menu without Directory Propagation.

With all nonnumeric selections, pressing Enter toggles through the possible answers or switches back and forth between Yes and No. To choose a selection requiring a number, press Enter, type the required number, and then press Enter again.

The eight settings under the Security profile determine password settings and access to DOS. These are the settings and what they control, with the defaults noted in parentheses:

Echo password: (Yes) When the user or administrator makes a change to a password, that word can be seen on the screen as it is typed. This does not affect the password for using cc:Mail. If set to No, the user does not see the password and must type it twice for confirmation.

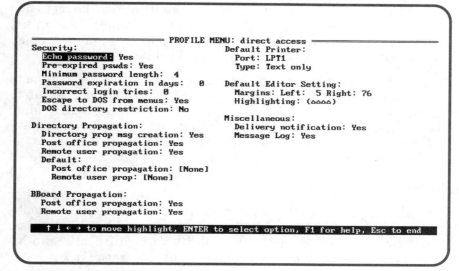

```
━━━━━━━━━━━━━━━ PROFILE MENU: direct access ━━━━━━━━━━━━━━━━
Security:                           Default Printer:
  Echo password: Yes                  Port: LPT1
  Pre-expired pswds: Yes              Type: Text only
  Minimum password length:  4
  Password expiration in days:   0  Default Editor Setting:
  Incorrect login tries:  0           Margins: Left:  5 Right: 76
  Escape to DOS from menus: Yes       Highlighting: (∆∆∆∆)
  DOS directory restriction: No
                                    Miscellaneous:
Directory Propagation:                Delivery notification: Yes
  Directory prop msg creation: Yes    Message Log: Yes
  Post office propagation: Yes
  Remote user propagation: Yes
  Default:
    Post office propagation: [None]
    Remote user prop: [None]

BBoard Propagation:
  Post office propagation: Yes
  Remote user propagation: Yes

┃  ↑ ↓ ← → to move highlight, ENTER to select option, F1 for help, Esc to end ┃
```

Figure 10.6   The Profile Menu with Directory Propagation installed.

201

Pre-expired pswds: (No) Normally the user enters the first password. If this setting is Yes, the user is provided with the password created by the administrator, which must be changed during the first cc:Mail session.

Minimum password length: (1) Any value from 1 to 10 determines the minimum length for passwords. A value of 0 makes a password optional.

Password expiration in days: (0) Users may be required to change their password every 1 to 365 days. A value of 0 does not require a password change. The change interval is based on the last date the password was changed.

Incorrect log-in tries: (0) To prevent password guessing, this value can be set from 1 to 99. Once the number of tries has been exceeded, the mailbox is locked and the administrator must change the password to unlock it.

Escape to DOS from menus: (Yes) Users can temporarily leave the cc:Mail menu and use DOS from any menu with the F9 key. Changing the setting to No prevents users from exiting to DOS from the menus.

DOS directory restriction: (No) With this setting, users can access directories above the cc:Mail directory to attach files. If this is set to Yes, users can access only the cc:Mail directory and subdirectories below it.

The Default Printer and Default Editor settings can be set in this profile but then changed by the users. For example, if the initial printer settings are based on the network printer, some users may decide to change these settings to a local printer.

The Miscellaneous settings relate to messages from remote users and maintenance of a Message Log folder. The only reason to change the Delivery Notification setting to No is if all cc:Mail Remote users are using version 3.2 or later. These later versions automatically provide a return receipt when a cc:Mail Remote user reads the message. A return receipt is automatically requested for all messages sent by cc:Remote users.

A Message Log setting of Yes allows users to create a folder named Message Log. All messages the user sends are then automatically copied to this special folder. The advantage for the user is a complete record of all messages sent. Changing this setting to No prevents the user from having an automatic Message Log.

202

User Support and Training

As the cc:Mail administrator, you are likely to have direct or indirect responsibility for user training and support. You may be responsible for providing support on more than just cc:Mail. Whether you have a well-staffed support desk or answer all the calls yourself, the basic training and support issues remain the same:

Keep users informed. If you have not initiated cc:Mail, let network users know when to expect the system and the advantages of using e-mail. Once cc:Mail is installed, let users know if features are being added and solicit ideas for bulletin board topics.

Schedule training sessions. Provide as much advance notice of training sessions as possible. Provide guidelines concerning who can benefit from the different levels of training.

Provide policy guidelines. Electronic mail represents a new and unique communications channel. Provide written documentation explaining password security, message privacy, and proper and improper use of the cc:Mail system.

Focus the support channel. cc:Mail provides its own support channel. Unless a user can't access his or her mailbox at all, many questions can be sent as a message. Make sure users know whom to send messages to or whom to call when they need help. Provide a quick response or return call if the answer warrants.

Be responsive to requests. Ask for and respond to requests for new bulletin boards or alias names. Let users know that everyone helps shape this communications channel.

Create a cc:Mail bulletin board to post general messages about the post office and system. Make sure important messages about the system are also broadcast to the entire mailing directory.

 What is the most important thing for cc:Mail administrators to do?

203

The most important function that an administrator can provide is preserving the stability of the system—that is, maintaining adequate backup of the databases, ensuring the integrity of the database, and keeping the system stable and operational. If any electronic system is not reliable, the users of the system will, if at all possible, quickly abandon it.

All e-mail administrators should make management aware not only of their operational procedures but also of the sensitive issues surrounding e-mail use and security. They should press for company-wide published policies regarding such things as proper and improper use. Company policies are important, especially regarding personal mail and mail privacy, and they need to include clearly spelled out guidelines as to who can and cannot gain legitimate access to the mail systems and why.

What You Have Learned

► Mailboxes are limited to the number of users purchased for cc:Mail. Other addresses such as aliases and post offices have no limit.

► Public mailing lists can be used by everyone in the post office. Consider how often a name appears on multiple lists.

► Bulletin boards are public folders for posting messages for everyone to read and use. Only the sender and administrator can delete bulletin board messages.

► The post office profile sets the level of security, the printer and editor defaults, and the ability of users to keep automatic message logs.

► For support to be effective, users must know where to get help and must receive that help as quickly as possible.

Programs for Administrators

In This Chapter

▶ *Determining message flow*
▶ *Restoring unused disk space*
▶ *Providing modem access to your post office*

The cc:Mail Platform Pack contains three programs that are useful for post office administration: Chkstat, Reclaim, and Dialin. Chkstat performs several functions, such as resetting pointers, showing system usage, and listing the directory. Reclaim recovers unused disk space. And Dialin allows cc:Mail users to access your post office with a modem and the cc:Mail Remote program.

Checking the Status: Chkstat

The cc:Mail database contains many links and cross-references between users and messages. The Chkstat program supplied with the Platform Pack provides statistics about the database, including message status and user activity. Chkstat can also correct discrepancies found in the database files.

> **Caution:** Users must not be using the cc:Mail post office while Chkstat DIAGNOSTICS is running. Make sure all users are locked out before running Chkstat with the DIAGNOSTICS parameter.

As an administrative tool, Chkstat is used only when you, the administrator, decide to run it. At a minimum, Chkstat should be run:

▶ before running the Reclaim program, which recovers empty disk space;

▶ before and after a version upgrade on the cc:Mail post office;

▶ on a regular schedule, depending on message volume, to check and maintain the integrity of the database.

206

If you want to observe the post office and determine how it is being used, you can use Chkstat in several ways:

▶ to determine the current message statistics, including the number of messages and the amount of disk space used by those messages;

▶ to compare the distribution of messages in user mailboxes and bulletin boards;

▶ to list all the users, including each user's location, last usage date, and address;

▶ to see if users are reading Inbox messages;

▶ to delete old messages by date in one or more areas of the post office.

Using Chkstat

The Chkstat program was copied to the administrative area of the system when the post office was first created. You must have access to that directory and know the post office name and password to run Chkstat. As noted in the Caution above, you must lock the mail system before running Chkstat with the DIAGNOSTICS parameter options.

The command line must include one or more of the following parameters: ADDRESSES, DIRECTORY, MESSAGES, USERS, and DIAGNOSTICS. You may also include the post office name, password, and location on that command line. For example, to run diagnostics on the post office, you might type:

CHKSTAT WIDGET-HQ BAT-NODE M:\CCDATA DIAGNOSTICS

If the post office name and password are not included in the command line, Chkstat prompts for them. If you do not add at least one parameter, the program issues an error message and returns you to the system prompt. Figure 11.1 shows this error message as well as the messages that follow a successful start of the program. You can use Esc at any time to terminate the program.

```
M:\CCADMIN>CHKSTAT WIDGET-HQ BAT-NODE M:\CCDATA
Statistics option required on command line.

M:\CCADMIN>CHKSTAT WIDGET-HQ BAT-NODE M:\CCDATA DIAGNOSTICS
Version 3.20  Copyright (c) 1991.  cc:Mail, Inc.  All rights reserved.

WARNING!  To run this program, you must have exclusive read and write access
          to the cc:Mail database.

Do you have exclusive access to the cc:Mail database (Y or N)?
```

207

Figure 11.1   Starting the Chkstat program.

Chkstat Command Parameters

Each of the five command parameters is independent of the others. For example, if you include DIRECTORY and ADDRESSES on the command line, you get the same results as when running Chkstat once with DIRECTORY and then again with ADDRESSES. All five main parameters can be run at the same time to produce one long report.

Of the five command parameters, DIAGNOSTICS, MESSAGES, and USERS can contain optional switches. How and when you use these depends on the type of information you need about your post office. The basic command parameters and their respective switches are listed below.

DIAGNOSTICS

This parameter checks the recorded count and actual count of items in the post office. If the numbers do not match, the administrator is prompted about whether or not to reconcile the difference.

/R

When /R is added to the end of the word DIAGNOSTICS, reconciliation is performed automatically. Chkstat also does not provide the first "exclusive access" prompt, as shown in Figure 11.1.

/L

The /L switch lists message details as each is examined by the DIAGNOSTICS function.

MESSAGES

This parameter examines and reports on the status of messages within the post office. If you use the switches below, you will limit your report to the specific areas. Otherwise, all users and bulletin boards will be included in the report.

/USER	Inboxes and folders
/BBOARD	bulletin boards
/READ	Inbox messages that have been read and all folders
/UNREAD	unread Inbox messages
/[mailbox]	a specified mailbox name (must be enclosed in brackets)
/[bboard]	a specified bulletin board name (must be enclosed in brackets)
/mm/dd/yy	all messages on or before specified date
/INBOX	all user Inboxes
/FOLDER	all user folders

/MSGLOG	all folders named Message Log
/DAYS/*n*	all messages older than *n* days
/DELETE	permanently deletes messages based on other criteria included in the command line

USERS

This parameter on the Chkstat command line provides a list of local users and post offices. The optional switches are as follows:

/N	lists all local and post office names alphabetically
/A	lists all local and remote users in the mailing directory
/A/N	lists the complete mailing directory sorted alphabetically

ADDRESSES

This parameter provides an alphabetical list of all addresses, including the location and cc:Mail address.

209

DIRECTORY

This report provides a list of addresses as they appear to the user, including the Comments column.

The screen output from the Chkstat program scrolls up the screen too quickly to read. However, two methods allow you to make a permanent copy of this information. To create a printed report as the program runs, press the Ctrl and PrtSc keys simultaneously just before typing and entering the command line. The contents of the screen will then be echoed to the printer. Press Ctrl and PrtSc again to turn this screen-to-printer echo off.

The information can also be sent to a text file with the DOS redirection symbol >. For example, you would type the following command to create and redirect a report to a file named WHO-LIST.TXT:

```
CHKSTAT WIDGET-HQ BAT-NODE M:\CCDATA DIRECTORY > WHO-LIST.TXT
```

After a brief delay, you would be returned to the system prompt. Then you could use a text editor to view the file or the DOS PRINT command to print the file. The information in the text file could also be used in many spreadsheet programs. By collecting this data on a specific schedule, you could also detect usage patterns.

> **Tip:** Because the DIAGNOSTICS parameter requires an initial response and possibly subsequent responses, use `DIAGNOSTICS/R` if you are capturing text to a file.

The DIAGNOSTICS Parameter

The DIAGNOSTICS parameter of the Chkstat program should be used regularly. When run, the program checks counters against actual entries. The areas checked include mailboxes, mailing lists, bulletin boards, and individual user files.

Unless the /R switch is added to the end of the parameter, the administrator is prompted with Reconcile? if a discrepancy is found. Unless otherwise advised by cc:Mail technical support, you should always respond with Y for yes. If you press any other key, the program continues without making the change.

> **Tip:** Use /R when creating a batch file line to run the Chkstat program automatically. This allows DIAGNOS-TICS to run without prompts. This is also helpful when you are capturing text to a file.

Figure 11.2 shows an abbreviated listing on the screen from the DIAGNOSTICS parameter. The bottom of the screen shows the prompt to reconcile a message pointer. In this case, the response was N for no. The command line was the following:

```
CHKSTAT WIDGET-HQ BAT-NODE M:\CCDATA DIAGNOSTICS
```

The /L parameter on DIAGNOSTICS displays a message header line as it is being checked. The information on this report includes the message number, sender, date, and some technical information. Much of the information from /L is useful only for diagnostic purposes.

The MESSAGES Parameter

Without additional parameters, the MESSAGES parameter provides a global view of messages in the post office. The report includes messages shared, messages not shared, the total message count, and the number of bytes for mailboxes and bulletin boards. Adding parameters restricts the report to the selected area or areas, depending on which parameters you use.

```
Mailbox counter: 21
Mailbox entries: 21

Mailing list counter: 5
Mailing list entries: 5
Mailing list: #ACQU/DEV EDITORS
Name counter: 2
Name entries: 2

Bulletin board counter: 6
Bulletin board entries: 6
Bulletin board: #CURRENT TITLES
Message counter: 1
Message entries: 1

Counting message pointers:
Reading USR00006...10
Reading USR00010...13

Msg #   PntCnt   UseCnt   Offset   Length   Sender           Date & Time Sent
   92        1        2    2ca00      400   Dan Derrick      7/18/91 9:43PM
Reconcile? N
No changes made.
134 message pointers verified.
M:\CCADMIN>
```

Figure 11.2   An abbreviated output screen from Chkstat.

For example, if you want to see which users are not reading their mail, you can see how many unread messages are sitting in Inboxes. The command line might be:

CHKSTAT WIDGET-HQ BAT-NODE M:\CCDATA MESSAGES/UNREAD/USER

Figure 11.3 shows the results of this example. In this case, Sally Daily has a total of six unread messages in her Inbox. As the system administrator, you may want to know why Sally is not using cc:Mail.

The /BBOARD parameter shows which bulletin boards are being used and the total size of the messages in each area. Figure 11.4 shows the results of the MESSAGES/BBOARD parameter.

```
Version 3.20  Copyright (c) 1991.  cc:Mail, Inc.  All rights reserved.


              cc:Mail Post Office: Widget-HQ
              Message Statistics: 7/25/91 2:08PM


Number of stored messages:      134
Total bytes in messages:    1852928
Total bytes remaining:      8455168
    Reclaimable bytes:        27648
    Additional bytes:       8427520

                    Not Shared        Shared            Total
  Mailbox Name      Msgs    Bytes    Msgs    Bytes    Msgs    Bytes

Blake, Linda          1      512      18   154624      19   155136
Daily, Sally          3    39936       3     1536       6    41472
Gage, Mary            1      512       3   226816       4   227328
Knight, Kathy         0        0       0        0       0        0
Royer, Molly          0        0       0        0       0        0
                  ------ --------   ------ --------   ------ --------
    Subtotal          5    40960      24   382976      29   423936

M:\CCADMIN>
```

Figure 11.3   *An unread Inbox message report from Chkstat.*

```
              cc:Mail Post Office: Widget-HQ
              Message Statistics: 7/25/91 2:16PM


Number of stored messages:      134
Total bytes in messages:    1852928
Total bytes remaining:      8453120
    Reclaimable bytes:        27648
    Additional bytes:       8425472


                    Not Shared        Shared            Total
  Bulletin Board    Msgs    Bytes    Msgs    Bytes    Msgs    Bytes

##Directory Updates   3     2048       0        0       3     2048
#AUTHORS              0        0       1   225792       1   225792
#CURRENT TITLES       0        0       1      512       1      512
#PRODUCTION SPECIFIC  0        0       0        0       0        0
#RESEARCH TOPICS      0        0       2     1024       2     1024
#TECH SUPPORT         0        0       1      512       1      512
                  ------ --------   ------ --------   ------ --------
    Subtotal          3     2048       5   227840       8   229888

M:\CCADMIN>
```

Figure 11.4   *A report on bulletin board usage.*

If you add the /DELETE option to the command line, the message database will be permanently altered. Using this option can have serious consequences. Therefore, before using /DELETE to recover disk space for new messages, you should take several steps to prevent the loss of critical data.

1. Inform users in advance that all messages older than a specific date will be deleted from the post office. This may include bulletin board messages as well as folders. Important messages created on or before that date should be archived to a disk file.

2. Just before using /DELETE, back up the database completely.

3. Use the command line to select the messages without /DELETE first. Make sure you are selecting the messages you want to delete. You may want to capture this report by redirecting it into a text file with a command such as > **0891DEL.TXT**, which you would add at the end of your command line.

4. Add the /DELETE option to the line to delete the messages. There is no prompt to confirm message deletion.

5. Use the command line again without /DELETE. The number of messages in all columns should be zero.

213

Figure 11.5 shows an abbreviated report using the following command line:

CHKSTAT WIDGET-HQ BAT-NODE M:\CCDATA MESSAGES/DAYS/45/USER

```
M:\CCADMIN>type 45DAYS


Version 3.20  Copyright (c) 1991.  cc:Mail, Inc.  All rights reserved.

                cc:Mail Post Office: Widget-HQ
                Message Statistics: 7/25/91 2:53PM
                Stored more than 45 days ago

                      Not Shared       Shared          Total
      Mailbox Name    Msgs    Bytes   Msgs    Bytes   Msgs    Bytes

      Blake, Linda      1      512     0       0       1       512
      Daniels, Erik     1      512     0       0       1       512
      Derrick, Dennis   0       0      0       0       0        0
      England, Steve    0       0      3      1536     3      1536
      Fellows, Mark     0       0      0       0       0        0
      Gage, Mary        1      512     0       0       1       512
                      ------ ------  ------ -------  ------ -------
        Subtotal        3     1536     3     1536     6      3072

M:\CCADMIN>
```

Figure 11.5   A report of user messages older than 45 days.

Notice that the report shows the number of days used in the command line. (A cutoff of 45 days is not at all standard.) Figure 11.6 shows the same report after the /DELETE option was added to the command line. As expected, those messages have been removed from the post office database.

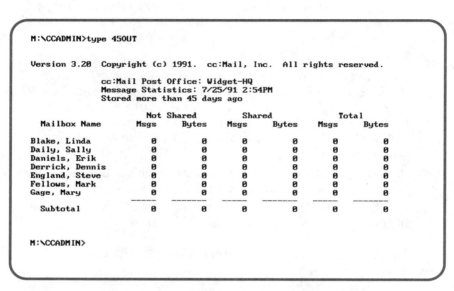

Figure 11.6 A report of user messages older than 45 days after using /DELETE.

The USERS Parameter

The USERS parameter should not be confused with the /USER option of the MESSAGES parameter. USERS provides a report on each user, including his or her location, the internal file number used by cc:Mail, and the number of bytes in that file. Without additional switches, the names are sorted by file number. If you add the /N option, however, the list is sorted by name. To list all users (everyone identified in the post office), include the /A option. You can also combine the /A and /N options to produce an alphabetical list of all the users. Figure 11.7 shows an abbreviated report generated with the USERS parameter.

```
Version 3.20  Copyright (c) 1991.  cc:Mail, Inc.  All rights reserved.

              cc:Mail Post Office: Widget-HQ
              User Statistics: 7/25/91 3:44PM

                                USR          File
     Mailbox Name      Locn     File #       Bytes
     Daniels, Erik     L        00001        3234
     Knight, Kathy     L        00002        1178
     Kathy             R        00003        1024
     Daily, Sally      L        00004        1348
     Royer, Molly      L        00005        1024
     Blake, Linda      R        00006        1842
     England, Steve    L        00008        5048
     Gage, Mary        L        00009        1330
     Childs, Harry     R        00010        1186
     Derrick, Dan      L        00011        2978
     Fellows, Mark     R        00014        1024
     FAX               P        00016        1348
     Fax-Administrator a        00018        1572
     Derrick, Dennis   R        00025        1024

     M:\CCADMIN>
```

Figure 11.7   A report on users generated by the USERS parameter.

215

The ADDRESSES and DIRECTORY Parameters

The ADDRESSES parameter of the Chkstat program indicates the number of remote post offices and remote mailboxes and displays user names, locations, and cc:Mail addresses. The DIRECTORY parameter lists user names, locations, the last date each used the system, and descriptive comments about the users. Figures 11.8 and 11.9 show abbreviated listings produced with these commands. Notice that the Comments column line on the DIRECTORY listing wraps to the next line when displayed on the screen.

Saving Disk Space: Reclaim

For the most part, the cc:Mail program manages disk space effectively by reusing the space that remains from deleted messages. Over time, however, small parts of the disk space cannot be used by the program. The Reclaim program reorganizes the entire database to eliminate that wasted space.

```
Version 3.20  Copyright (c) 1991.  cc:Mail, Inc.  All rights reserved.

            cc:Mail Post Office: Widget-HQ
            cc:Mail Addresses: 7/25/91 3:19PM

Remote post offices:      4
Remote mailboxes:        10

   Mailbox Name              Locn    cc:Mail Address

Blake, Linda                  R     Widget-HQ
Childs, Harry                 R     Widget-HQ
Daily, Sally                  L     Widget-HQ
Daniels, Erik                 L     Widget-HQ
England, Steve                L     Widget-HQ
FAX                           P     FAXLINK
Gage, Mary                    L     Widget-HQ
Holmes, Ron                   r     Wayne FAX
Kathy                         R     Widget-HQ Knight, Kathy
Knight, Kathy                 L     Widget-HQ
Mailroom                      a     Derrick, Dan
Molly                         a     Royer, Molly
Royer, Molly                  L     Widget-HQ

M:\CCADMIN>
```

Figure 11.8   An abbreviated report generated by the ADDRESS parameter.

```
Version 3.20  Copyright (c) 1991.  cc:Mail, Inc.  All rights reserved.

            cc:Mail Post Office: Widget-HQ
            Directory: 7/25/91 3:21PM

Maximum local mailboxes: 9

Total mailboxes:      21
    Local:            7
    Remote:          14

   Mailbox Name          Locn    Last Checked In       Comments

Blake, Linda              R     7/16/91 2:11PM      Editor
Daily, Sally              L     6/11/91 1:52PM      Editorial Assistant
Daniels, Erik             L     7/24/91 3:00PM      Author
England, Steve            L     7/24/91 6:49AM      Acquisitions/Developmen
t Editor
FAX                       P     7/25/91 9:06AM      FAXLINK
Fax-Administrator         a
Gage, Mary                L     6/11/91 12:13PM     Acquisitions/Developmen
t Editor
Knight, Kathy             L     7/21/91 12:48PM     New name
Royer, Molly              L                         Account Manager
M:\CCADMIN>
```

Figure 11.9   An abbreviated report generated by the DIRECTORY parameter.

> **Caution:** Before using Reclaim you must lock all users
> out of the post office and run Chkstat DIAGNOSTICS.

You should run the Reclaim program when one or more of the
following conditions occur:

► You've upgraded your copy of cc:Mail.

► You have less than 10 percent of the allocated space free for
  your post office files.

► A number of changes to the mail directory have been made.

► The total database size exceeds the message size by 15
  percent. (Compare Msg Bytes and Data Base on the Main
  menu screen of Admin. You have to calculate the percentage.)

► You have not used Reclaim for two or more weeks.

► If the MLANDATA file grows more than two megabytes in
  size per day, use Reclaim more frequently.

► If your post office is a routing hub, use reclaim more
  frequently.

217

The Reclaim Command Line

The cc:Mail database contains two database files, CLANDATA and
MLANDATA, as well as the user files USRxxxxx. Reclaim copies the
existing files to new files as part of the reorganization. The program
must have enough space for those new copies in the current
directory. If there is not enough space, you must add parameters to
the command line so that the new files can be copied elsewhere in
the system or so that only a part of the database is reorganized.

The Reclaim command line contains the same information
used for the Admin program: the post office, the password, and the
location of the post office files. For example, the Reclaim command
line might be:

```
RECLAIM WIDGET-HQ BAT-NODE M:\CCDATA
```

Figure 11.10 shows the results of running Reclaim. Each line
represents a step in the process. The final line indicates that the
reorganization succeeded.

```
Version 3.20 Copyright (c) 1991.  cc:Mail, Inc.  All rights reserved.
Press Esc to terminate RECLAIM program.

WARNING!  To run this program, you must have exclusive read and write access
          to the cc:Mail database.

Reorganizing cc:Mail user file m:\ccdata\USR00006 on drive m:\ccdata\
Reorganizing cc:Mail user file m:\ccdata\USR00010 on drive m:\ccdata\
Reorganizing cc:Mail user file m:\ccdata\USR00004 on drive m:\ccdata\
Reorganizing cc:Mail user file m:\ccdata\USR00001 on drive m:\ccdata\
Reorganizing cc:Mail user file m:\ccdata\USR00011 on drive m:\ccdata\
Reorganizing cc:Mail user file m:\ccdata\USR00025 on drive m:\ccdata\
Reorganizing cc:Mail user file m:\ccdata\USR00008 on drive m:\ccdata\
Reorganizing cc:Mail user file m:\ccdata\USR00016 on drive m:\ccdata\
Reorganizing cc:Mail user file m:\ccdata\USR00018 on drive m:\ccdata\
Reorganizing cc:Mail user file m:\ccdata\USR00014 on drive m:\ccdata\
Reorganizing cc:Mail user file m:\ccdata\USR00009 on drive m:\ccdata\
Reorganizing cc:Mail user file m:\ccdata\USR00003 on drive m:\ccdata\
Reorganizing cc:Mail user file m:\ccdata\USR00002 on drive m:\ccdata\
Reorganizing cc:Mail user file m:\ccdata\USR00005 on drive m:\ccdata\
Reorganizing cc:Mail database file m:\ccdata\CLANDATA on drive m:\ccdata\
Reorganizing cc:Mail database file m:\ccdata\MLANDATA on drive m:\ccdata\
Reclaim process successful.

M:\CCADMIN>
```

218

Figure 11.10   Messages generated by Reclaim.

Additional parameters on this line can include a different drive, USERS, DIRECTORY, MESSAGES, and RENAME. The different drive would be used only if there is not enough space to duplicate the files on the current drive. In this case, you must use standard system commands to copy the database files from the target file back to the original database file.

The USERS, DIRECTORY, and MESSAGES parameters reorganize only their respective parts of the database. As a result, Reclaim requires less disk space when you use these parameters.

The RENAME parameter prevents users from accessing the post office during the reorganization. The main data file, CLANDATA, is renamed CLANORIG as soon as Reclaim is run. Once Reclaim is successful, the original files are erased and the new files are renamed to the original names. If you cannot control access to the data files, the RENAME parameter is the best way to prevent accidental access to the post office while it is being reorganized.

Remote Access: Dialin

cc:Mail generally runs on a network server that also contains the post office database. Callers outside of the network can access the post office with cc:Mail Remote and a modem. (cc:Mail Remote is covered in Chapter 8, "Using cc:Mail Remote.") One program that receives calls from cc:Mail Remote is Dialin, which is included with the Platform Pack.

Dialin requires a dedicated system attached to the network that contains a modem and uses one direct phone line. If remote users are to be able to send and receive messages anytime, the system must run the Dialin program full time. If remote users call and exchange messages only at certain times, Dialin could be run during those scheduled hours.

Dialin can accept one call at a time from a local user, a remote user, a receive-only caller, or a cc:Mail Gateway program. In all four cases, the call must be initiated from the outside. Unlike Gateway, Dialin does not initiate calls to other post offices to exchange messages. (Gateway is covered in Chapter 12, "Additional cc:Mail Programs.")

219

A local user with a mailbox in the post office can send and receive mail remotely. Once the modem connection is made, the Inbox messages are transmitted to be read on the remote system. These local messages are marked as having been read but are left in the Inbox. This assumes the caller will return to the office at some point to finish handling the messages. Messages can be replied to and forwarded just as though the user is on the network, except that the transactions do not actually take place until the next call to the post office.

A remote user does not have a local Inbox. The only way these users can send and receive mail is with the cc:Mail Remote program. Their names are placed in the directory by the administrator. When they call in, all messages they have are transmitted from their computers to the post office. Any messages addressed to them in the post office are sent to their local computers during the call. Remote users maintain all their messages on their remote computers.

A receive-only (R/O) caller can only send messages to the post office. To send a message, the caller must know the post office phone number, a name, and a mailbox in the post office directory. Once the caller makes the connection, the system determines that he or she does not have an address in the directory. Since the system accepts messages only for names in the directory, the name on the message must match in order for the Dialin program to accept the message.

Dialin can accept calls and exchange messages with the cc:Mail Gateway program. To exchange messages, the name must have been entered as a remote user with the Dialin post office name as the address. As noted, the call must still be initiated from the other system with Gateway.

In all cases, the remote user must maintain the remote mailing directory by entering the post office name, phone number, and directory names. In this respect, the remote user is like an administrator who maintains the directory list.

To run Dialin successfully you need to have some knowledge of telecommunications. First of all, you should test the modem and phone connection with a standard communications program. Once Dialin is running, you should reduce frustration for remote callers by testing the program with another computer equipped with a modem and cc:Mail Remote.

Dialin Command Line

During installation, Dialin was copied to the administrative directory, typically \CCADMIN. The minimum required to start Dialin is the program name and the post office location. For example, after you change to the CCADMIN directory, the command line could be:

```
DIALIN M:\CCDATA
```

Notice that the post office name or password is not required. This command line assumes that your system has a modem attached to COM1: and runs at 1200 baud. The modem may be attached to another COM port and, more typically, run at 2400 baud. To adjust for these differences, add these parameters to the command line. For example, if the modem is an internal modem on COM3: and runs as 2400 baud, the command line would be:

```
DIALIN M:\CCDATA COM3 2400
```

Once loaded, Dialin resets the modem. The message Waiting to receive messages... then appears on the screen. As calls are accepted and messages sent and received, the screen displays the transactions. Figure 11.11 shows some Dialin transaction messages.

```
M:\CCADMIN>dialin m:\ccdata com3 2400
Version 3.20  Copyright (c) 1991.  cc:Mail, Inc.   All rights reserved.
Press Esc to terminate cc:Mail DIALIN program.
7/25/91 8:28PM Answering call from Dan Derrick.   Accepted connection.
Receiving message.  Unknown recipients.
0 messages received.
0 messages sent.
7/25/91 8:28PM Hanging up telephone.  On-hook.
7/25/91 8:31PM Answering call from Dan Derrick.   Accepted connection.
1 message received.
0 messages sent.
7/25/91 8:32PM Hanging up telephone.  On-hook.
7/25/91 8:35PM Answering call from Dan Derrick.   Accepted connection.
0 messages received.
1 message sent.
7/25/91 8:35PM Hanging up telephone.  On-hook.
7/25/91 8:37PM Answering call from Dan Derrick.   Accepted connection.
1 message received.
0 messages sent.
7/25/91 8:37PM Hanging up telephone.  On-hook.
Waiting to receive messages...
```

221

Figure 11.11   Some Dialin transaction messages.

The Dialin command line can include over a dozen other parameters for your additional communication needs. The DIAGNOSTICS parameter on the command line echoes all modem command characters to the screen. This helps determine if the modem is responding to the commands initiated by Dialin.

If a system is not dedicated to Dialin full time, the END parameter on the command line can return the system to other tasks. For example, if the system also performs an automatic tape backup of the host, a batch file called DIALGO.BAT might include the following:

```
REM DIALGO.BAT
DIALIN M:\CCDATA COM3 2400 END/2:00AM
TAPEBACK F: M:
DIALGO
```

In this sample batch file, the Dialin program would end at 2:00 a.m. The Tapeback program would run to back up drives F: and M:. Then the batch file would run again, with Dialin waiting for more calls.

What You Have Learned

► You should run Chkstat with the DIAGNOSTICS parameter on a regular basis to perform housekeeping on the post office.

► Chkstat can help you determine how the cc:Mail system is being used.

► You can list addresses in several different ways with the Chkstat parameters USERS, ADDRESSES, and DIRECTORY.

► Reclaim recovers unused disk space in the post office data files.

► Dialin allows outside access to your post office with a modem and cc:Mail Remote.

Additional cc:Mail Programs

In This Chapter

▶ *Exchanging messages with other post offices*
▶ *Updating remote mailing directories*
▶ *Linking with other e-mail services*

A cc:Mail community may contain as few as nine local mailboxes from one Platform Pack and one 8 User Pack or as many as thousands of users spread across the world. In order to link different locations and different post offices, however, you need additional software from cc:Mail. The Gateway program provides this connection for multiple post offices and users. For directory updates, another product, Automatic Directory Exchange, keeps every post office current with names from all other post offices.

   With additional software, cc:Mail can also branch to different e-mail systems such as PROFS, MCI Mail, SMTP, and X.400. The first connection point for many of these systems is the cc:Mail Gateway program. Gateway is not required for X.400 and SMTP conntectivity.

Gateway

Gateway sends cc:Mail messages to other post offices in different locations or within the same network. A computer with a modem and dedicated direct phone line runs the Gateway program to distribute messages to and receive messages from other post offices. Depending on their design, the other systems may also use Gateway or just the Dialin program supplied with the Platform Pack.

With Gateway running on the cc:Mail system, users can exchange messages with any name in the directory, whether the person is in the next office or across the country. You, the system administrator, and Gateway provide the hidden links between all the users in the cc:Mail community. The messages are routed based on the call list and schedule you establish in Gateway.

One Gateway system can be the hub of the mail exchange. All messages are then sent to the hub and back out to the outlying post offices. Or each post office can be independent, running Gateway and calling other post offices only when mail needs to be delivered.

In addition to Gateway, you'll need a computer system with a modem and dedicated direct phone line to establish a link to post offices outside your network. For testing purposes, use cc:Mail Remote to determine that your Gateway program answers calls and transmits messages successfully.

Installation

To install the Gateway programs, you need to copy the program files to a suitable location on the network host. These files can be copied to the same directory as Admin or to their own directory. Unless you want users to initiate a Gateway call on their own, access should be restricted to an administrative level.

Before you can establish a connection with other post offices, you must take several steps:

▶ Get the post office name and phone number and the name of someone at another post office.

▶ Use Admin to add that information to the post office directory.

224

► Use Gtwadmin to place that post office on the call list.

► After testing the modem and phone line, run Gateway.

Even before you run Gateway, you must create the directory listing by using the Admin program. Until now you may have had local and remote users. Now you'll add a new type of address: post office. The post office name you enter in the directory must exactly match the name at the other post office. If it does not, the receiving system will not accept your call. In addition to the post office name, you must have the post office phone number and at least one name in that directory.

With this information, you can use Admin to create two new entries. The first contains the post office name (with a location of P for post office) and address, which is same as the phone number. The second entry contains the mailbox in that post office. In the address line, you enter the post office name.

Take, for example, a post office named DA-WEST at 1-317-555-1212. The DA-WEST post office has a user named Harry Jones. His mailbox line would be Jones, Harry, with the address of DA-WEST. When someone selects Harry Jones to send mail, Gateway has Harry's address as the DA-WEST post office and sends the message.

The Gateway package contains two programs, Gateway and Gtwadmin. After running Admin to insert the new post office and mailbox address, you must run Gtwadmin to place that post office on the call table. You also establish default call intervals, the number of retries, the retry interval, and the call password.

Gtwadmin is run just like Admin. The command line requires the post office location and can include the post office name and password. If these are provided on the command line, the Main menu immediately appears. For example, the command line might be:

```
GTWADMIN DA-HQ BAT-NODE M:\CCDATA
```

Figure 12.1 shows the main screen in Gtwadmin. The upper portion of the screen provides statistics related to the call entries, call profile, and post office. The profile and post office information can be changed from this Main menu.

225

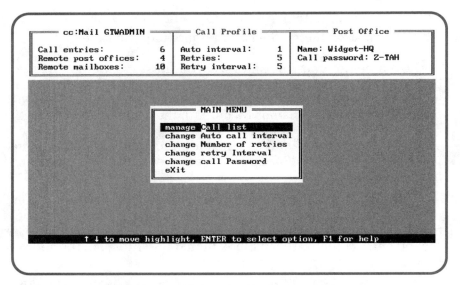

Figure 12.1   The Gtwadmin opening screen.

Creating the Call List

The call list controls which post offices are called and when. Figure 12.2 shows a sample Call List screen and the Call List menu. These names and post offices must appear in the directory before they can be added to this list. To enter a new line, you first type the time when the call to this entry will be made.

Once the time has been entered, the Mailing Directory list appears. Select the post office from this list. Once selected, the prompt returns to Add new call time or select existing entry:. To change the other columns in this call list, you must select the existing entry. The Call List menu then appears as shown in Figure 12.2.

Each post office can be called according to its own parameters. You use the Call List menu to choose these settings. Many of the settings also affect other settings. For example, priority level is affected by message size. Consider all the settings when changing even one.

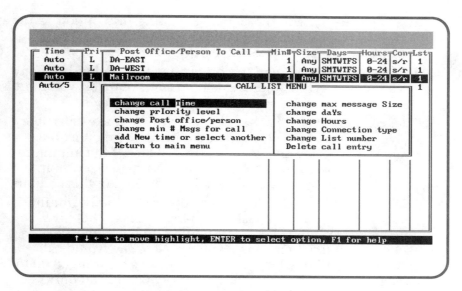

Figure 12.2   The Gtwadmin Call List menu.

change call Time   This changes the call interval for an automatic call to Auto or Auto/n, where n equals minutes between calls. The time may also be expressed as hh:mm on the 24-hour clock or in a.m. and p.m. For example, 23:00 and 11:00PM are both valid entries. The program changes 23:00 to 11:00PM in this column.

change prIority level   The default of L for Low priority sends all messages. If the priority is higher, either N for Normal or U for Urgent, those messages are sent first.

change Post office/person   This replaces the current value with another selected from the directory.

change min # Msgs for call   The default of 1 means that a call to a post office is made only if there is a message waiting to be delivered. To reduce the number of phone connections, enter a higher number. Once that number of messages has been reached, the post office is called, and all the messages are delivered. To call regularly at the time interval, set this value to 0. With this setting, any waiting messages are picked up from the other post office. This might be necessary if your post office serves as a hub system for a number of slaves using Dialin.

add New time or select another Selecting this option is the same as pressing Esc. You return to the Add new call time... prompt.

change max message Size If you change this option from Any to a number, which represents thousands of bytes, you limit the size of messages sent or received during a call.

change daYs The call schedule default is to make calls every day. Days may be deleted from the lineup by moving the cursor to that day and pressing the Del key. If the minimum number of messages is set to 0 to call for message pickup, Saturday and Sunday could easily be deleted in this column.

change Hours The hours column represents the beginning and ending time when Gateway makes calls to that post office. For example, if the minimum number of messages is set as 0 and the interval is one hour, Gateway would call every hour, all day long. If the bracket was set from 08:00 to 17:00 (8:00 a.m. to 5:00 p.m.), Gateway would call only during those hours.

change Connection type The default of Send/receive allows the post office to send and receive messages during a call. Changing this to send only or receive only limits the transaction to one or the other direction.

change List number If multiple Gateway programs are running on the same network server, each entry must be assigned by call list number. The default is 1.

Delete call entry After a Yes/No prompt, the call list entry is deleted. To replace that entry, you enter it as a new line.

Return to main menu This option returns you to the Main menu. Pressing Esc also returns to this menu.

Changing the Profile

Four of the remaining five choices on the Gtwadmin program set default values for the post office. With the exception of the password, these values can be changed at any time. The fifth menu selection, eXit, returns you to the operating system.

change Auto call interval When a post office is entered on the call list, you can specify how often that post office is to be called. If you use Auto for the time, the value set will be determined by this menu choice. The current value is displayed at the top of the screen under the Call Profile. The value may range from 1 to 1440 minutes (one day).

change Number of retries If the receiving post office is busy or for some other reason does not accept the call, you can set the number of times Gateway attempts to make the connection.

change retry Interval This value sets the number of minutes Gateway is to pause between retries.

change call Password For a post office to exchange messages with yours, it must know your password. Initially this password is the same as your post office access password. If you don't change it, other administrators can access your post office directly. If you change the call password later, you must inform all other post office administrators.

229

 Caution: You should change the Gateway call password immediately after installing the Gateway program.

Running Gateway

Once you have used Admin to enter post offices in the mailing directory and Gtwadmin to add these post offices to the call list, you are ready to run Gateway. At the minimum, the command line needs only the program name and the location of the post office. For example, the command line might be:

```
GATEWAY M:\CCDATA
```

Notice that the post office name or password is not required. This command line assumes that your system has a modem attached to COM1: and runs at 1200 baud. The modem may be attached to another COM port and, more typically, run at 2400 baud. To adjust for these differences, add these parameters to the command line. For example, if the modem is an internal modem on COM3: and runs at 2400 baud, the command line would be:

GATEWAY M:\CCDATA COM3 2400

Once loaded, Gateway resets the modem. Once set, the message Next call at 8:00AM. Waiting to receive messages... appears on the screen. (The actual time depends on the time of day Gateway was started.) The time changes on the screen based on the call list. As calls are accepted and messages sent and received, the screen displays the transactions. Figure 12.3 shows some sample Gateway transaction messages.

```
M:\GATETEMP>m:\ccadmin\gateway m:\ccdata com3 2400
Version 3.20 Copyright (c) 1991.  cc:Mail, Inc.  All
  rights reserved.
Press Esc to terminate cc:Mail Gateway program.
7/24/91 1:04PM Placing call to DA-EAST.  Data
  connection not accepted.
7/24/91 1:05PM Hanging up telephone.  On-hook.
7/24/91 1:05PM Placing call to DA-WEST.  Call not
  established.
7/24/91 1:11PM Placing call to DA-EAST.  Connection
  accepted.
1 message sent.
0 messages received.
7/24/91 1:13PM Hanging up telephone.  On-hook.
7/24/91 1:13PM Placing call to DA-WEST.  R/O
  connection accepted.
1 message sent.
0 messages received.
7/24/91 1:15PM Hanging up telephone.  On-hook.
```

Figure 12.3   Gateway transactions.

The Gateway command line can include over two dozen other parameters to meet additional communication needs. These parameters include setting the COM: port and the modem speed, sending initialization strings to the modem, using batch files and scripts, and generating a log file.

The ability to record Gateway transactions can help you, the administrator, monitor the message traffic. To create an ASCII file of each transaction, add the parameter LOG/ followed by the filename for the log file. For example, to start a log file called GATE01.LOG, the command line might be:

```
GATEWAY M:\CCDATA LOG/GATE01.LOG COM3 2400
```

> **Caution:** Although the file can be examined at any time, if it is loaded into a word processing program or other program, a sharing violation may result that will prevent Gateway from writing to the file. To use the file while Gateway is still active, make a copy of the file and examine the copy.

The log file contains extensive information on each transaction, including the date, time, post office, number of characters sent and received, and error codes generated. This file is in a standard data format and can be used in any program that imports ASCII SDF.

231

Gateway Express Mode

Gateway can also be used to send messages immediately to a specific post office. To do this, users must have access to the Gateway program and a modem on their computer. The advantage to this approach is immediate delivery of messages; the disadvantage may be unexpected phone charges.

All the startup parameters are available in the Express mode. In addition, the post office name must also be included on the command line. Assuming the user has a 2400-baud modem on COM2:, the command line for an immediate exchange of messages between the local post office and DA-WEST would be:

```
GATEWAY DA-WEST M:\CCDATA COM2 2400
```

Gateway would immediately call the DA-WEST post office and exchange messages. Incoming messages would be placed in the appropriate Inbox in the local post office. The user would then use cc:Mail normally to read and respond to any messages.

Automatic Directory Exchange

Each post office has its own mailing directory of users. Once a cc:Mail community grows beyond the local post office, however, that post office is likely to include users located at other post offices. Although the users do not need to know the addresses of other mailboxes, the administrator does need to coordinate the exchange of mailboxes and addresses with other post offices.

The Directory Exchange, also known as Directory Propagation, automates this process. Once installed, the administrator makes selections in the Admin profile to determine the types of exchanges for mailing lists and bulletin boards. Figure 12.4 shows the Admin Profile screen with Directory Propagation installed.

232

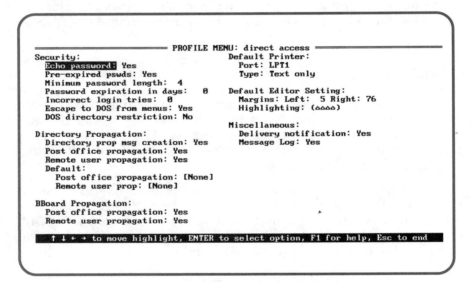

Figure 12.4   A post office profile with Directory Exchange.

The directory information may be exchanged or just transmitted in one direction. This exchange depends on the type of peer-to-peer or master-slave post office network.

E-Mail Links

Additional software packages allow Gateway to transmit messages to other electronic mail systems. These connections include cc:Mail Link to X.400, SMTP, MCI Mail, PROFS, Soft*Switch, Telelink, and EZLink. Additional information about the first three systems is provided here.

MCI Mail

MCI Mail services include messages to other MCI Mail subscribers, REMS (Remote Electronic Mail Systems), fax, and messages printed and delivered by courier. Users prepare and send messages to mailboxes in the mailing directory. The MCI Mail Link then sends the message to the MCI Mail services through the REMS account established by the administrator. The administrator can specify what MCI services are available to users in the post office and when message transmissions are to occur.

233

SMTP

The Simple Mail Transfer Protocol (SMTP) link provides access to UNIX, Bitnet, and PROFS as well as any mail system based on this protocol. The link includes all TCP/IP and FTP software required for a PC, which convert messages to the proper incoming or outgoing format. An Ethernet card connected to the TCP/IP Ethernet network is required to complete the connection.

X.400

The link to X.400 also provides transparent connections to X.400 mail systems worldwide. Messages are routed through the Retix OpenServer 400 via X.25, 802.3, 802.5, ISDN, FDDI, and public or private Wide Area Networks (WAN). Nearly all addressing features are supported, including Subject, Priority, Copy, and Blind Copy. A few X.400 features, such as Expiration Date, are not supported. A Retix OpenServer 400 MH-411 configured as a LAN workstation is required in addition to the cc:Mail Link to X.400 compliant software.

What You Have Learned

▶ Gateway provides an outside link with other post offices by means of a modem and phone line.

▶ To install Gateway you need to create post office addresses with Admin and then add them to the Gateway call table with Gtwadmin.

▶ The call list entries can be scheduled by time of day, time interval, or the number of messages to be sent.

▶ The post office profile includes the post office password and the call password. The password allows you to access the post office locally. The call password allows other post offices to exchange messages.

▶ To send messages to another post office, you must have at least one name of a mailbox on that system.

234

▶ The Directory Exchange can update each post office mailing directory automatically based on the administrator's choices.

▶ cc:Mail provides a number of software packages to link to other electronic mail services.

Issues and Concepts for the Administrator

The cc:Mail Platform Pack installs itself after you provide answers to several questions. Before you install the software and implement an e-mail system, however, you need to consider a number of issues.

Even if you are already familiar with the basic issues involved in running an e-mail system, you may still find this review beneficial. If you have limited experience as a system administrator, you should take these concepts seriously as a sound basis for maintaining an effective system.

Learn the Basics

The host computer has all copies of all the program and database files. You control access to the database and administrative programs by limiting access to those areas of the disk. Each user profile is maintained on the host in the database area.

The directory names recommended by cc:Mail and the main files contained in those directories are shown in Table A.1. The users need only have access to the CCMAIL and CCDATA directories in order to use the cc:Mail system. The administrator needs access to all three areas. These directories are created as the default by the installation program.

Table A.1   *Directories and Files.*

CCADMIN	CCDATA	CCMAIL
ADMIN.EXE	CLANDATA	MAIL.EXE
CHKSTAT.EXE	MLANDATA	MESSENGR.EXE
RECLAIM.EXE	MAIL.HLP	NOTIFY.COM
DIALIN.EXE	ADMIN.HLP	SNAPSHOT.EXE
	USRxxxxx	

Once a user's name has been entered as part of the mailing directory, the user runs Mail to access the system. His or her profile is maintained in a file named USRxxxxx, the final five characters of which are a unique number.

The database files in the CCDATA directory are the heart of the system. On the network, users send messages to each other with Mail or Messenger. They can exchange messages with other post offices through Gateway. They can call in with cc:Mail Remote to read, respond, and handle their mail. Everything depends on these database files.

Test the System

As with any network installation, install and test the programs thoroughly before opening the programs up to users. If you are not familiar with the program or e-mail concepts, you can install the Platform Pack on a single system and test the process of sending and receiving mail before installing the software on the network. Since the Platform Pack provides for only one user, you'll have to send and receive messages to and from yourself. Before conducting this test installation, you must run the DOS SHARE program.

Grow Slowly

Although the network design may call for an extensive Wide Area Network (WAN) of post offices, start small. Create a post office with several dozen users. Provide orientation and training and take time to discover where you need to fine-tune the system. If you plan to use Gateway or Dialin for remote users, let several people try the system from home in the evening. This tests their ability to make all the proper connections from a remote location. Problems can be resolved and the system tested again the next night.

Nothing will doom an e-mail system to failure more quickly than major problems that occur during the first month the system is installed. If messages are lost or the system is too slow to handle the traffic, users will return to whatever communication channels they used before the "new, improved electronic mail" was introduced.

The main problems with developing an effective e-mail system may well relate less to hardware and software and more to people. Unless everyone uses the system, it will not work. Talk to users in the test group and see why they did or did not use the system. Then adjust the training and support to accommodate those needs.

Establish Policies

Above all, prepare and distribute clear guidelines for using the e-mail system. Everyone must know who has access to the messages and why such access might be necessary. If the company determines that all mail is proprietary, the users must know that what they send may not remain private. Although this may seem harsh, recent court cases have brought these issues to light.

Provide users with guidelines for bulletin board messages. Define what is appropriate and what is not. If the organizational structure is well established, explain in detail that, although you can easily send a message to the company president, protocol dictates communication via the chain of command.

Distribute this document to all cc:Mail users. Remember to keep it to as few pages as possible. You may want to consider attaching it to copies of this book. Introduce the policy document in the training session once the users are comfortable with the basics of cc:Mail.

Provide Support

Publish support phone numbers and provide local support people. Make sure someone from each work group knows about and is enthusiastic about e-mail. Only by providing quick answers to e-mail questions can you convince users to take the time to learn the new system. And only by seeing others use the system successfully will new users understand the benefits of electronic communication.

238

Keep the System Operational

Consider how much you would or would not use the telephone if you could place calls only every other day. A reliable system for delivering messages is essential if e-mail is to become effective in an organization.

If, for some reason, the system is not working as it should or you anticipate the system being down (this applies to the network as well), let users know what happened or what is about to happen. Although you can use the power of a company-wide mailing list to provide this information, you should consider using other channels as well. Otherwise, less-frequent users may not receive the original message and may find that the system is down when they expect to use it. As a result, they may never try again.

Index

240

241

243

244

Sams—Covering The Latest In Computer And Technical Topics!

Audio

Audio Production Techniques for Video	$29.95
Audio Systems Design and Installation	$59.95
Audio Technology Fundamentals	$24.95
Compact Disc Troubleshooting and Repair	$24.95
Handbook for Sound Engineers: The New Audio Cyclopedia	$79.95
Introduction to Professional Recording Techniques	$29.95
Modern Recording Techniques, 3rd Ed.	$29.95
Principles of Digital Audio, 2nd Ed.	$29.95
Sound Recording Handbook	$49.95
Sound System Engineering, 2nd Ed.	$49.95

Electricity/Electronics

Basic AC Circuits	$29.95
Electricity 1, Revised 2nd Ed.	$14.95
Electricity 1-7, Revised 2nd Ed.	$49.95
Electricity 2, Revised 2nd Ed.	$14.95
Electricity 3, Revised 2nd Ed.	$14.95
Electricity 4, Revised 2nd Ed.	$14.95
Electricity 5, Revised 2nd Ed.	$14.95
Electricity 6, Revised 2nd Ed.	$14.95
Electricity 7, Revised 2nd Ed.	$14.95
Electronics 1-7, Revised 2nd Ed.	$49.95

Electronics Technical

Active-Filter Cookbook	$19.95
Camcorder Survival Guide	$ 9.95
CMOS Cookbook, 2nd Ed.	$24.95
Design of OP-AMP Circuits with Experiments	$19.95
Design of Phase-Locked Loop Circuits with Experiments	$19.95
Electrical Test Equipment	$19.95
Electrical Wiring	$19.95
How to Read Schematics, 4th Ed.	$19.95
IC Op-Amp Cookbook, 3rd Ed.	$24.95
IC Timer Cookbook, 2nd Ed.	$19.95
IC User's Casebook	$19.95
Radio Handbook, 23rd Ed.	$39.95
Radio Operator's License Q&A Manual, 11th Ed.	$24.95
RF Circuit Design	$24.95
Transformers and Motors	$24.95
TTL Cookbook	$19.95
Undergrounding Electric Lines	$14.95
Understanding Telephone Electronics, 2nd Ed.	$19.95
VCR Troubleshooting & Repair Guide	$19.95
Video Scrambling & Descrambling for Satellite & Cable TV	$19.95

Games

Beyond the Nintendo Masters	$ 9.95
Mastering Nintendo Video Games II	$ 9.95
Tricks of the Nintendo Masters	$ 9.95
VideoGames & Computer Entertainment Complete Guide to Nintendo Video Games	$ 9.50
Winner's Guide to Nintendo Game Boy	$ 9.95
Winner's Guide to Sega Genesis	$ 9.95

Hardware/Technical

Hard Disk Power with the Jamsa Disk Utilities	$39.95
IBM PC Advanced Troubleshooting & Repair	$24.95
IBM Personal Computer Troubleshooting & Repair	$24.95
IBM Personal Computer Upgrade Guide	$24.95
Microcomputer Troubleshooting & Repair	$24.95
Understanding Communications Systems, 2nd Ed.	$19.95
Understanding Data Communications, 2nd Ed.	$19.95
Understanding FAX and Electronic Mail	$19.95
Understanding Fiber Optics	$19.95

IBM: Business

Best Book of Microsoft Works for the PC, 2nd Ed.	$24.95
Best Book of PFS: First Choice	$24.95
Best Book of Professional Write and File	$22.95
First Book of Fastback Plus	$16.95
First Book of Norton Utilities	$16.95
First Book of Personal Computing	$16.95
First Book of PROCOMM PLUS	$16.95

IBM: Database

Best Book of Paradox 3	$27.95
dBASE III Plus Programmer's Reference Guide	$24.95
dBASE IV Programmer's Reference Guide	$24.95
First Book of Paradox 3	$16.95
Mastering ORACLE Featuring ORACLE's SQL Standard	$24.95

IBM: Graphics/Desktop Publishing

Best Book of Autodesk Animator	$29.95
Best Book of Harvard Graphics	$24.95
First Book of DrawPerfect	$16.95
First Book of Harvard Graphics	$16.95
First Book of PC Paintbrush	$16.95
First Book of PFS: First Publisher	$16.95

IBM: Spreadsheets/Financial

Best Book of Lotus 1-2-3 Release 3.1	$27.95
Best Book of Lotus 1-2-3, Release 2.2, 3rd Ed.	$26.95
Best Book of Peachtree Complete III	$24.95
First Book of Lotus 1-2-3, Release 2.2	$16.95
First Book of Lotus 1-2-3/G	$16.95
First Book of Microsoft Excel for the PC	$16.95
Lotus 1-2-3: Step-by-Step	$24.95

IBM: Word Processing

Best Book of Microsoft Word 5	$24.95
Best Book of Microsoft Word for Windows	$24.95
Best Book of WordPerfect 5.1	$26.95
Best Book of WordPerfect Version 5.0	$24.95
First Book of PC Write	$16.95
First Book of WordPerfect 5.1	$16.95
WordPerfect 5.1: Step-by-Step	$24.95

Macintosh/Apple

Best Book of AppleWorks	$24.95
Best Book of MacWrite II	$24.95
Best Book of Microsoft Word for the Macintosh	$24.95
Macintosh Printer Secrets	$34.95
Macintosh Repair & Upgrade Secrets	$34.95
Macintosh Revealed, Expanding the Toolbox, Vol. 4	$29.95
Macintosh Revealed, Mastering the Toolbox, Vol. 3	$29.95
Macintosh Revealed, Programming with the Toolbox, Vol. 2, 2nd Ed.	$29.95
Macintosh Revealed, Unlocking the Toolbox, Vol. 1, 2nd Ed.	$29.95
Using ORACLE with HyperCard	$24.95

Operating Systems/Networking

Best Book of DESQview	$24.95
Best Book of DOS	$24.95
Best Book of Microsoft Windows 3	$24.95
Business Guide to Local Area Networks	$24.95
Exploring the UNIX System, 2nd Ed.	$29.95
First Book of DeskMate	$16.95
First Book of Microsoft QuickPascal	$16.95
First Book of MS-DOS	$16.95
First Book of UNIX	$16.95
Interfacing to the IBM Personal Computer, 2nd Ed.	$24.95
Mastering NetWare	$29.95
The Waite Group's Discovering MS-DOS	$19.95
The Waite Group's Inside XENIX	$29.95
The Waite Group's MS-DOS Bible, 3rd Ed.	$24.95
The Waite Group's MS-DOS Developer's Guide, 2nd Ed.	$29.95
The Waite Group's Tricks of the MS-DOS Masters, 2nd Ed.	$29.95
The Waite Group's Tricks of the UNIX Masters	$29.95
The Waite Group's Understanding MS-DOS, 2nd Ed.	$19.95
The Waite Group's UNIX Primer Plus, 2nd Ed.	$29.95
The Waite Group's UNIX System V Bible	$29.95
The Waite Group's UNIX System V Primer, Revised Ed.	$29.95
Understanding Local Area Networks, 2nd Ed.	$24.95

Understanding NetWare	$24.95
UNIX Applications Programming: Mastering the Shell	$29.95
UNIX Networking	$29.95
UNIX Shell Programming, Revised Ed.	$29.95
UNIX System Administration	$29.95
UNIX System Security	$34.95
UNIX Text Processing	$29.95
UNIX: Step-by-Step	$29.95

Professional/Reference

Data Communications, Networks, and Systems	$39.95
Gallium Arsenide Technology, Volume II	$69.95
Handbook of Computer-Communications Standards, Vol. 1, 2nd Ed.	$39.95
Handbook of Computer-Communications Standards, Vol. 2, 2nd Ed.	$39.95
Handbook of Computer-Communications Standards, Vol. 3, 2nd Ed.	$39.95
Handbook of Electronics Tables and Formulas, 6th Ed.	$24.95
ISDN, DECnet, and SNA Communications	$44.95
Modern Dictionary of Electronics, 6th Ed.	$39.95
Programmable Logic Designer's Guide	$29.95
Reference Data for Engineers: Radio, Electronics, Computer, and Communications, 7th Ed.	$99.95
Surface-Mount Technology for PC Board Design	$49.95
World Satellite Almanac, 2nd Ed.	$39.95

Programming

Advanced C: Tips and Techniques	$29.95
C Programmer's Guide to NetBIOS	$29.95
C Programmer's Guide to Serial Communications	$29.95
Commodore 64 Programmer's Reference Guide	$19.95
DOS Batch File Power	$39.95
First Book of GW-BASIC	$16.95
How to Write Macintosh Software, 2nd Ed.	$29.95
Mastering Turbo Assembler	$29.95
Mastering Turbo Debugger	$29.95
Mastering Turbo Pascal 5.5, 3rd Ed.	$29.95
Microsoft QuickBASIC Programmer's Reference	$29.95
Programming in ANSI C	$29.95
Programming in C, Revised Ed.	$29.95
QuickC Programming	$29.95
The Waite Group's BASIC Programming Primer, 2nd Ed.	$24.95
The Waite Group's C Programming Using Turbo C++	$29.95
The Waite Group's C++ Programming	$24.95
The Waite Group's C: Step-by-Step	$29.95
The Waite Group's GW-BASIC Primer Plus	$24.95
The Waite Group's Microsoft C Bible, 2nd Ed.	$29.95
The Waite Group's Microsoft C Programming for the PC, 2nd Ed.	$29.95
The Waite Group's Microsoft Macro Assembler Bible	$29.95
The Waite Group's New C Primer Plus	$29.95
The Waite Group's QuickC Bible	$29.95
The Waite Group's Turbo Assembler Bible	$29.95
The Waite Group's Turbo C Bible	$29.95
The Waite Group's Turbo C Programming for the PC, Revised Ed.	$29.95
The Waite Group's TWG Turbo C++Bible	$29.95
X Window System Programming	$29.95

For More Information, Call Toll Free

1-800-257-5755

All prices are subject to change without notice.
Non-U.S. prices may be higher. Printed in the U.S.A.

Sams Keeps You Up-To-Date
With The Most Current DOS Titles

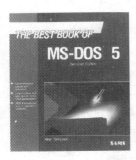

Sams' Series Puts You "In Business"

The *In Business* books have been specially designed to help business users increase their productivity and efficiency. Each book comes with a companion disk that contains templates for common business tasks, as well as tear-out quick references for common commands. In addition, the books feature Business Shortcuts—boxed notes and tips on how to improve the performance of the software. Regardless of the size of the business or the level of user, these books will teach you how to get the most out of your business applications.

Quattro Pro 3 In Business
Chris Van Buren
400 pages, 7 3/8 x 9 1/4, $29.95 USA
0-672-22793-2

Lotus 1-2-3 Release 2.3 In Business
Michael Griffin
400 pages, 7 3/8 x 9 1/4, $29.95 USA
0-672-22803-3

Harvard Graphics 2.3 In Business
Jean Jacobson & Steve Jacobson
400 pages, 7 3/8 x 9 1/4, $29.95 USA
0-672-22834-3

Q&A 4 In Business
David B. Adams
400 pages, 7 3/8 x 9 1/4, $29.95 USA
0-672-22801-7

WordPerfect 5.1 In Business
Neil Salkind
400 pages, 7 3/8 x 9 1/4, $29.95 USA
0-672-22795-9

SAMS

See your local retailer or call 1-800-428-5331.

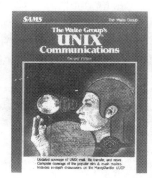

Reader Feedback Card

Thank you for purchasing this book from SAMS FIRST BOOK series. Our intent with this series is to bring you timely, authoritative information that you can reference quickly and easily. You can help us by taking a minute to complete and return this card. We appreciate your comments and will use the information to better serve your needs.

1. Where did you purchase this book?

☐ Chain bookstore (Walden, B. Dalton)   ☐ Direct mail
☐ Independent bookstore   ☐ Book club
☐ Computer/Software store   ☐ School bookstore
☐ Other _____

2. Why did you choose this book? (Check as many as apply.)

☐ Price   ☐ Appearance of book
☐ Author's reputation   ☐ SAMS' reputation
☐ Quick and easy treatment of subject   ☐ Only book available on subject

3. How do you use this book? (Check as many as apply.)

☐ As a supplement to the product manual   ☐ As a reference
☐ In place of the product manual   ☐ At home
☐ For self-instruction   ☐ At work

4. Please rate this book in the categories below. G = Good; N = Needs improvement; U = Category is unimportant.

☐ Price   ☐ Appearance
☐ Amount of information   ☐ Accuracy
☐ Examples   ☐ Quick Steps
☐ Inside cover reference   ☐ Second color
☐ Table of contents   ☐ Index
☐ Tips and cautions   ☐ Illustrations
☐ Length of book
☐ How can we improve this book? _____
☐

5. How many computer books do you normally buy in a year?

☐ 1–5   ☐ 5–10   ☐ More than 10
☐ I rarely purchase more than one book on a subject.
☐ I may purchase a beginning and an advanced book on the same subject.
☐ I may purchase several books on particular subjects.
☐ (such as _____)

6. Have your purchased other SAMS or Hayden books in the past year? _____
If yes, how many _____

7. Would you purchase another book in the FIRST BOOK series? _____

8. What are your primary areas of interest in business software? _____

☐ Word processing (particularly _____)
☐ Spreadsheet (particularly _____)
☐ Database (particularly _____)
☐ Graphics (particularly _____)
☐ Personal finance/accounting (particularly _____)
☐ Other (please specify _____)

Other comments on this book or the SAMS' book line: _____
_____

Name _____
Company _____
Address _____
City _____ State _____ Zip _____
Daytime telephone number _____
Title of this book _____

Fold here

- -